W9-BOL-494

# Katy Perry

*Purposeful Pop Icon*

By Vanessa Oswald

Portions of this book originally appeared in
*Katy Perry* by Anne K. Brown.

LUCENT
P R E S S

Published in 2019 by
**Lucent Press, an Imprint of Greenhaven Publishing, LLC**
353 3rd Avenue
Suite 255
New York, NY 10010

Designer: Deanna Paternostro
Editor: Vanessa Oswald

**Library of Congress Cataloging-in-Publication Data**

Names: Oswald, Vanessa, author.
Title: Katy Perry : purposeful pop icon / by Vanessa Oswald.
Description: New York : Lucent Press, [2019] | Series: People in the news |
   Includes bibliographical references and index.
Identifiers: LCCN 2017055796| ISBN 9781534563247
   (library bound book) | ISBN 9781534563230 (pbk. book) |
   ISBN 9781534563254 (ebook)
Subjects: LCSH: Perry, Katy–Juvenile literature. | Singers–United
   States–Biography–Juvenile literature.
Classification: LCC ML3930.P455 O89 2019 | DDC 782.42164092 [B] –dc23
LC record available at https://lccn.loc.gov/2017055796

Printed in the United States of America

CPSIA compliance information: Batch #BS18KL: For further information contact Greenhaven Publishing LLC, New York,
New York at 1-844-317-7404.

Please visit our website, www.greenhavenpublishing.com. For a free color
catalog of all our high-quality books, call toll free 1-844-317-7404 or fax
1-844-317-7405.

# Contents

# Foreword

We live in a world where the latest news is always available and where it seems we have unlimited access to the lives of the people in the news. Entire television networks are devoted to news about politics, sports, and entertainment. Social media has allowed people to have an unprecedented level of interaction with celebrities. We have more information at our fingertips than ever before. However, how much do we really know about the people we see on television news programs, social media feeds, and magazine covers?

Despite the constant stream of news, the full stories behind the lives of some of the world's most newsworthy men and women are often unknown. Who was Katy Perry before she was a pop music phenomenon? What does LeBron James do when he's not playing basketball? What inspires Lin-Manuel Miranda?

This series aims to answer questions like these about some of the biggest names in pop culture, sports, politics, and technology. While the subjects of this series come from all walks of life and areas of expertise, they share a common magnetism that has made them all captivating figures in the public eye. They have shaped the world in some unique way, and—in many cases—they are poised to continue to shape the world for many years to come.

These biographies are not just a collection of basic facts. They tell compelling stories that show how each figure grew to become a powerful public personality. Each book aims to paint a complete, realistic picture of its subject—from the challenges they overcame to the controversies they caused. In doing so, each book reinforces the idea that even the most famous faces on the news are real people who are much more complex than we are often shown in brief video clips or sound bites. Readers are also reminded that there is even more to a person than what they present to the world through social media posts, press releases, and interviews. The whole story of a person's life can only be discovered by digging beneath the surface of their public persona, and that is what this series allows readers to do.

The books in this series are filled with enlightening quotes from speeches and interviews given by the subjects, as well as quotes and anecdotes from those who know their story best: family, friends, coaches, and colleagues. All quotes are noted to provide guidance for further research. Detailed lists of additional resources are also included, as are timelines, indexes, and unique photographs. These text features come together to enhance the reading experience and encourage readers to dive deeper into the stories of these influential men and women.

Fame can be fleeting, but the subjects featured in this series have real staying power. They have fundamentally impacted their respective fields and have achieved great success through hard work and true talent. They are men and women defined by their accomplishments, and they are often seen as role models for the next generation. They have left their mark on the world in a major way, and their stories are meant to inspire readers to leave their mark, too.

# An Unconventional Pop Star

Katy Perry's first attempts at launching her music career were met with confusion from executives at record companies. Many saw her potential and agreed she had genuine talent, but her style was unlike anything they had seen before. Her songs did not fit into any traditional musical categories. Executives did not know what to do with her music or how to sell it to the public. As a result, Perry's career had a number of false starts and stalled opportunities.

Perry knew that other musicians, such as Alanis Morissette and Gwen Stefani, had experienced similar problems. Their music and image did not fit mainstream pop music, yet these women did not alter their music or personal style to fit the expectations of record companies. They stayed true to themselves while refusing to give up and pushed for a record deal until their dreams came true. Inspired by these women, Perry stuck to these principles as she fought for a music career of her own.

## From Plain Jane to Glamour Queen

Perry grew up in a conservative Christian household where she was not allowed to listen to the kind of music she now creates. She also was not allowed to wear the kinds of fashions for which she is now famous or watch the kinds of programs she has been featured on. Though loving and supportive, the community she grew up in was not made up of the diverse range of people with whom she now regularly interacts. According to Perry, her childhood was sheltered.

Her religious upbringing led her first to Nashville, Tennessee, to test her talents in the Christian music industry, then to Los Angeles, California, where she discovered an entirely new world of music and fashion. She experimented with different styles for several years

Katy Perry refused to give up, despite the adversity she faced when trying to get a record deal.

and after much hard work and some disappointment, eventually evolved into a pop star who has sold millions of records, appeared on award shows, and fascinated the public with her successful career.

Perry has been accused of many things throughout the years—of selling out her religious roots in favor of fame; of inventing crazy fashions and writing controversial lyrics for attention; and of being the invention of her producers rather than her own self. Reporters and critics have wondered how a teenage Christian musician could transform into a boundary-breaking pop star. Meanwhile, she has attracted anger from Christian conservatives and LGBT+ groups over two of her most controversial songs, "Ur So Gay" and "I Kissed a Girl."

Perry argues that she is really being true to her creative instincts and that she is more than just a string of publicity stunts. "You can't just change your dress or change your hair," she said. "That can't just be the basis of success. It has to spawn from something more powerful. It has to spawn from talent, you know?"[1] Perry's talent involves her vocal abilities, songwriting, and creation of an outrageous and unique style that always changes. Perry is particularly known for taking sweet, feminine, and fun styles to an extreme place. Some of these elaborate styles include fake food covered in sequins, carnival colors, light-up dresses, or candy-covered clothes. Her performances are just as creative as her fashions. For example, she has performed on giant gold dice, in a giant hand, and in a boxing ring. Her fashions sometimes draw criticism, but Perry also has kept the public in suspense, wondering what she will be wearing or how she will be performing at her next appearance.

## Staying True to Herself

Despite Perry's transformation from a humble Christian singer to an outrageous pop star, Perry feels she is the same person she has always been. She said she simply needed time to figure out and explore her true personality. She revealed to an interviewer that she often feels like the same girl who first moved to Los Angeles. "I think I'm not exactly what I was born into, but I still have my roots,"[2] she said.

Katy Perry continues to thrive and stand out in the world of pop music.

Since the start of her music career in 2001 as Katy Hudson, Perry has faced her fair share of ups and downs. Perry has been presented with many opportunities; some of them have back-fired for her, while others have brought her exceptional fame and praise. With the 2017 release of her fifth album, *Witness*, Perry worked to balance remaining one of the most sought-after pop artists of her generation with creating what she has called "purposeful pop," which is pop music with a message about social and political issues.

Through dealing with her personal relationships, whether they involve her significant others, friends, or business associates, she has learned a lot, and these personal highs and downfalls have inspired her in life and in her music. She is also not afraid to show her vulnerable side, which makes her relatable to ordinary people. As she shuffles between failures and successes, just like everyone else, she shows no signs of backing down from a challenge.

# Chapter **One**

## Sheltered Life to Cultural Exposure

**G**rowing up with her family in Santa Barbara, California, was vastly different compared to the life Katy Perry currently lives. Having represented the West Coast in her song "California Gurls," Perry has not failed to recognize where she comes from. However, as an adult, Perry now lives her life on her own terms, instead of following the morals of her parents.

### *Katheryn Hudson*

Katy Perry, whose full birth name is Katheryn Elizabeth Hudson, was born in Santa Barbara on October 25, 1984. Her mother and father, Keith and Mary Hudson, are both Christian ministers who carried their religion into every aspect of family life. Katy, along with her older sister, Angela, and younger brother, David, went to church several times a week and attended the Christian school affiliated with their Evangelical church. Each summer, they attended Christian camp.

Matters of religion were never open for debate in Katy's family. As Evangelical Christians, her parents believed they were following the only correct religion and the only one that would lead them to heaven. According to Katy's parents and their church, followers of other religions were on the wrong path and would not be accepted into heaven.

Katy's community was strict about living a clean lifestyle. Children were allowed to listen only to Christian music, never rock or pop. Their movie choices were limited to films that reflected family values—no swearing, sex, or violence. As a child, Katy accepted these rules and views easily, since everyone in her world shared her family's beliefs. Katy recalled, "Everyone related to me in my circle was from church: church friends, church school, church activities. All my friends weren't allowed to watch MTV or go to PG-13 movies or listen to the radio, so I didn't really know anything different. That's how I was raised."[3]

Despite their differences in opinions, Katy Perry loves her family (shown here with her) and occasionally attends events with them.

## A New World of Music and Dance

When Katy was nine years old, she began to sing in the church choir, as did many of her friends. She showed a great interest and talent in music and took voice lessons from several different teachers. When she was 13, she received her first guitar. She continued to sing at church until she was 16 years old.

Dance also became a hobby of Katy's. She took dance lessons

# **Religious** Upbringing

A number of Christian denominations, including the Evangelical faith that Katy Perry was raised in, exist in the United States. These include Catholic, Lutheran, and Episcopalian. Each denomination varies in its beliefs and practices. Some consider the Bible as a source of wisdom and inspiration, while others believe it must be obeyed word for word—not simply for the spirit of its messages, but precisely as it is written.

Evangelical Christianity exists in many different forms and varies from one church to the next. It is generally distinguished from other Christian denominations by its requirement of members to spread God's message throughout the world. Evangelicals will often approach friends, coworkers, or strangers to talk to them about God and invite them to worship services. They are also known for taking the Bible literally. Whereas some Christians consider certain Bible passages to be stories for the purpose of a lesson, many Evangelicals believe instead that those events happened exactly as written.

Like Katy's family, many Evangelical Christians take a conservative approach to life. They may limit their exposure to certain types of books, movies, and music and restrict their interaction with certain groups of people who do not share their beliefs.

at the Santa Barbara recreation center, where she learned the jitterbug, Lindy Hop, and swing dancing—dance styles from the 1920s, 1930s, and 1940s. The instructors and other dancers made an impression on her. "These girls would get out of their old vintage Cadillacs with their pencil skirts and their tight little cardigans ... and I thought it was so unique and different than what was going on in the 2000s,"[4] Katy recalled.

## Exposed to Culture

Despite her parents' efforts to shelter their children from pop culture, Katy sometimes discovered music that was beyond her approved boundaries. She recalled one musical influence that did not win approval from the adults in her life: "There was Alanis Morissette. [The album] *Jagged Little Pill* was huge for me. One of the vivid memories of my childhood is swinging on the swing set singing 'Ironic' at the top of my lungs. I went to Christian school, so I got into a little trouble for that one."[5]

Another one of Katy's musical influences was Freddie Mercury, lead singer of the rock band Queen. The band enjoyed popularity in the 1970s and 1980s. Although Mercury passed away in 1991 when Katy was only seven years old, his music still had an impact on her. She explained,

> *He was a turning point. I wasn't allowed to listen to secular music when I was [a] kid, but there was a time when I was hanging out at my friend's house. We're trying on all our outfits, like girls do, and out of nowhere I heard the lyrics to "Killer Queen." Time stood still. The music was totally different from anything I'd heard. I still love Freddie Mercury. He was flamboyant with a twist of the operatic.*[6]

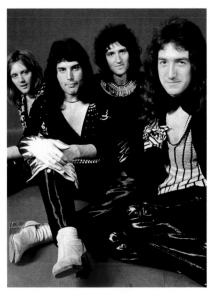

Freddie Mercury (second from left) of Queen was one of Katy Perry's biggest musical inspirations when she was growing up.

Other glimpses of the world outside Katy's clean-cut home life came during a few trips to Manhattan, New York, to visit her uncle, Frank Perry, who was a director on about 20 films during his career. His most famous production was *Mommie Dearest*, which was based on film legend Joan Crawford. Katy remembered one of her most vivid memories of those visits: "We would go to my uncle's apartment and see the drag queens [men dressed as women] in his neighborhood … That's New York to me."[7]

## *From Dress-Up to Skateboarding*

Katy loved to play dress-up and showed an interest in fashion from a young age. "I was always into dressing up, even when I was a little girl," she recalled. "My mom says I would wear a different outfit for breakfast, lunch, and dinner. It was my way of saying I wanted to *arrive*."[8]

Katy also displayed a different side to her personality. She took up skateboarding when she was 13 years old and for a while, did not mind a few scrapes and bruises. "As soon as Santa Barbara got a skate park, I was there after school every day,"[9] she said. Eventually, she abandoned skateboarding for safer hobbies, as she explained, "A friend of mine … was so good that she ended up going pro. I wasn't quite so good, but I could easily handle a half-pipe, where you're skateboarding almost vertically. I gave it up because I was scuffing my knees too much and I didn't like the idea of breaking bones."[10]

## *Music Career Aspirations*

After graduating from her Christian school, Katy attended Dos Pueblos High School in nearby Goleta, California. During the first semester of her freshman year, she decided to drop out of school and pursue a music career. She then passed her General Educational Development (GED) test, which gave her the equivalent of a high school diploma.

Around the same time, Katy began to rebel against her carefully controlled Christian upbringing. She started drinking and before long, threatened to spiral out of control. "I started spending Sunday mornings crying and hung over," she said. "Because crying is what you *do* when you're hung over."[11]

Katy Perry performed for students at Dos Pueblos High School in Goleta, California, on September 14, 2010.

During this time, Katy learned some surprising details about her parents' backgrounds. Her mother and father had not always lived the clean lifestyle that she had been brought up to respect. Both had gone through wild phases of their own when they were younger. For example, her father had used and sold lysergic acid diethylamide (LSD). Katy's father told her about his mistakes to show her she could escape making similar ones. Both her parents became religious at a time when they were taking part in dangerous behaviors. Katy learned that this probably saved her father from dying of a drug overdose and allowed her parents to settle into a healthy, cleaner lifestyle. "They needed to find God … God found them, really,"[12] she said of her parents' transformation.

## Networking in Nashville

Katy's love of music helped her to focus. Her parents knew some people in the Christian music industry, and she took advantage of those connections to meet people and look for auditions. When she was 15, she caught the attention of a group of musicians from Nashville, Tennessee, who asked her to visit them and learn more about songwriting and recording. She spent about a year traveling back and forth from Nashville to Santa Barbara. "That's when I started recording and meeting people and learned how to write a song, craft it, play my guitar better. It was like my school of

# Killer Queen

Chief among Katy Perry's musical role models was Freddie Mercury. He was born on September 5, 1946, on the island of Zanzibar. His parents were of Persian descent, and his birth name was Farrokh Bulsara. He was sent to boarding school in India from 1955 to 1963. His family then moved to England. Farrokh, who began calling himself Freddie as a teenager, graduated from the Ealing College of Art in 1969.

In 1970, Mercury became lead singer of a band called Smile; the name later changed to Queen. At the same time, Farrokh changed his name to Freddie Mercury. Queen's big break came in 1974 when the album *Sheer Heart Attack* was released. The album includes the song "Killer Queen," which was a major hit. A year later, the song "Bohemian Rhapsody" brought more fame to the group and became one of Queen's most famous songs. Queen and Freddie Mercury brought a unique sound to the music world. The group's songs had the feel of rock music but incorporated elements of orchestra and opera. Freddie Mercury died on November 24, 1991.

Freddie Mercury was the lead singer of Queen from 1970 to 1991.

rock,"[13] she said. She signed a contract to record an album with Red Hill Records and felt certain that her career was underway.

Life in Nashville was an adjustment for teenage Katy. Nashville is known for its glitzy country music scene and the famous Grand Ole Opry concert hall that has hosted the legends of country music. Katy's time in Nashville, however, was far from glamorous. She was an unknown artist—and she had a lot to learn. That did not scare her, and she worked hard to absorb everything she could from her environment. "I started going to Nashville to record some gospel songs, and to be around amazing country-music [veterans] and learn how to craft a song," she said. "I'd actually have to Superglue the tips of my fingers because they hurt so much from playing guitar all day, you know? And from that, I made the best record I could make as a gospel singer at 15."[14]

In 2001, when Katy was 16 years old, her first album was released. Titled *Katy Hudson*, it was categorized as a Christian gospel album. The album features 10 songs with names that subtly hint at Christian themes: "Trust in Me," "Piercing," and "Search Me" are among some of the tracks on the album, which also features "Last Call," "Growing Pains," "My Own Monster," "Spit," "Faith Won't Fail," "Naturally," and "When There's Nothing Left." Katy wrote four of the songs and co-wrote the other six songs on her album—an unusual accomplishment for a teenage singer.

Katy's album received only a few reviews but all had positive comments. A review by Russ Breimeier on the website Christianity Today described her style as alternative pop-rock and praised her songwriting ability, especially for someone so young. Breimeier also gave Katy credit for mixing different styles of music as well as producing an authentic sound. Katy's admiration of Freddie Mercury was noticed by Breimeier, who wrote, "The award for the most unique track goes to 'Growing Pains,' which has a goofy but artsy feel similar to Queen's 'Bohemian Rhapsody.'" He continued, "I hear a remarkable young talent emerging, a gifted songwriter in her own right who will almost certainly go far in this business. That name again is Katy Hudson. Trust me, you'll be hearing it more and more in the next year."[15]

# A **Big** Inspiration

Born in Canada on June 1, 1974, Alanis Morissette has earned international fame as an alternative rock star. She released two dance-pop albums in Canada as a teenager. Like Katy Perry, she moved to Los Angeles to expand her music career before she turned 20.

Several years ahead of Perry, Morissette worked with Glen Ballard to produce songs and land a recording contract. They had a difficult time finding a record company that would back her album. Eventually, Maverick Records took on Morissette and released *Jagged Little Pill*. When the album came out in June 1995, Morissette's team hoped it would sell 250,000 copies. Two months later, however, the album was given a gold album award after selling 500,000 copies, and a platinum award for selling 1 million copies. The album sold so fast that it won gold and platinum awards simultaneously. In July 1998, *Jagged Little Pill* reached diamond album

Katy's album also received praise in the United Kingdom (UK). A reviewer for the British Christian radio website Cross Rhythms remarked, "Katy clearly is a real vocal talent and the breathtaking fact that she's a mere 16 years old suggests a major star in the making."[16]

## Taking Risks

Katy's excitement over the release of her debut album would not last long. At the end of 2001, her record company, Red Hill Records, went bankrupt and closed permanently. Her album practically vanished. "It reached literally maybe 100 people … and then the label went bankrupt," she said. "It was not like I status (10 million copies sold). More than 20 years after the album's release, the *Jagged Little Pill* musical is set to debut in Cambridge, Massachusetts, and the team that is creating it is hoping to also bring it to Broadway in New York City.

Both Morissette and Perry were raised in strict religious households but have gained recognition as artists who speak their minds and do not shy away from controversial topics.

Alanis Morissette was one of Katy Perry's most influential musical role models.

was Amy Grant [a major Christian pop singer] or something. So I went back home."[17]

The setback would not be the end of Katy's career; the young musician was not easily deterred. She said, "I was just like, 'OK, well this is over. What do I do now?'"[18] She remembers watching VH1 one night, and Glen Ballard appeared on the screen. Ballard was a music producer and songwriter famous for bringing new artists to popularity. He had launched the career of early 1990s girl group Wilson Phillips, and his most successful production at that time was Alanis Morissette's album *Jagged Little Pill*. It is the same album that contains the song "Ironic," which Katy had gotten into trouble for singing as a young girl. Under Ballard's direction, *Jagged Little Pill* had won Grammy Awards for

Glen Ballard, shown here in 2002 with Katy Perry, took a chance on the young teenager when others did not know how to market her music. He was able to help bring her to popularity.

Best Rock Album and Album of the Year in 1996. Katy recalled she listened to Ballard discuss Morissette's *Jagged Little Pill* "and I was like, 'Well, that's a really good record. She speaks from my perspective. I want to make a record like that!'"[19]

Through some of her contacts in the music business, Katy managed to schedule an interview with Ballard. Upon hearing her sing, Ballard made up his mind almost immediately. He recalled, "She played the song and it was OK, that's all I need to know." The next day, he phoned Katy, who remembered he said, "I want to move you to Los Angeles. I want to help fulfill your dreams."[20]

Katy's parents understood her desire for a music career, but they had mixed feelings about her making a move to Los Angeles at such a young age. They ultimately gave Katy permission to move, and at the age of 17, with big dreams and her guitar in hand, Katy packed up her car and moved to Los Angeles.

# Chapter Two

# The Unpredictable Music Industry

**W**hen Katy Perry moved to Los Angeles, her whole world broadened and changed. She was introduced to an abundance of choices, which were not directly influenced by her conservative Christian community. For the first time, she had the freedom to form her own views about the various aspects of society. This enlightened perspective marked a brand new start for the artist. Her days as a gospel singer were behind her, and she began building her new identity.

Having separated herself from the influence of her conservative Christian community, she discovered new music, movies, people, fashions, and pop culture every day. As she said in a 2009 interview,

> When I started out in my gospel music my perspective then was a bit enclosed and very strict, and everything I had in my life at that time was very church-related. I didn't know there was another world that existed beyond that. So when I left home and saw all of that, it was like, "Omigosh, I fell down the rabbit hole and there's this whole Alice in Wonderland right there!"[21]

As Perry adjusted to life in Los Angeles and discovered a new sense of freedom, she continued to learn more about herself.

She discovered personal tastes in music and fashion that she had never known. She also realized that the rules she had grown up with did not apply to the rest of the world. "Letting go [of my past] was a process," she said. "Meeting gay people, or Jewish people, and realizing that they were fine was a big part of it. Once I stopped being chaperoned, and realized I had a choice in life, I was like, 'Wow, there are a lot of choices.' I began to become a sponge for all that I had missed—the music, the movies. I was as curious as the cat."[22]

## Accepting the Challenge

In Los Angeles, Perry went straight to work with Glen Ballard. He challenged her to develop her songwriting and performance skills by writing a song every day. He also encouraged her to experiment with different kinds of music and to find her true style. Meanwhile, Perry sang in small clubs to gain exposure.

Ballard tried hard to sign Perry to a number of record companies. For more than a year, he could not persuade anyone to take a chance on her. "We tried so many labels ... But you know, it was the same with Alanis: Everybody turned her down," Ballard remembered. "I think Katy was just maybe too ahead of her time."[23]

Around this time, Perry decided to adopt a stage name. She worried the name Katy Hudson might lead people to confuse her with the actress Kate Hudson. For that reason, she adopted the name Katy Perry, using her mother's maiden name as her new last name.

Perry was working hard at her music career and also to make ends meet. Money was tight, and she had to depend on her parents for help. Living in fast-paced Los Angeles, Perry fell into a partying lifestyle and began drinking heavily again. At one point, she realized what she was doing to herself, as she explained: "Drinking became a problem. It got out of control until I said, *Ok—back to work.*"[24] She knew she had to get serious if she wanted to succeed.

Eventually, Ballard's persistence paid off. He landed a record deal for Perry with Island Def Jam Music Group. Her album was slated for release in 2005; however, she was still a long way from success. "The first time I got signed, they brought me in a room with three other girls they signed at the same time," she recalled. "They sat us down and said, 'Maybe *one* of you will ever make a record … The other three can go back to middle America.'"[25] Perry took those words as a challenge. She got busy writing, recording, and dreaming of the day her album would be released.

## A New Opportunity

In 2004, while working toward the release of her own album, a new break came for 19-year-old Perry. She was recruited by a production team called the Matrix to perform as part of a new group. The team consisted of Lauren Christy, Graham Edwards, and Scott Spock. This team had written songs for Avril Lavigne and helped launch her career in 2002.

The Matrix's new project was to be an album with Columbia Records featuring Christy, Edwards, Spock, and new talent to round out the band. A newcomer, British singer Adam Longlands, was brought into the group, and Perry was chosen to complete the quintet as lead singer.

The album, which was to be titled *The Matrix*, was a major investment for the team. It was produced at great expense, along with music videos. The Matrix production team began a marketing campaign to promote the upcoming release. Then, only a few weeks before the album's launch in September 2004, the entire project was canceled.

Perry worked alongside Lauren Christy (left) while she waited for the release of her solo album.

Perry was disappointed—but also relieved. The style of the Matrix did not really fit her own personal tastes. "I had this kind of quirky, unique perspective, and they had a very mainstream-pop perspective, which was really cool, too, but I wasn't used to it. We made a record that sonically sounds brilliant but doesn't say much … My own stuff is very heart-on-my-sleeve."[26] The Matrix team released the album in 2009; Perry requested for them to wait until the fourth single off of her album *One of the Boys* was released.

## A Flicker of Good News

Perry still had a goal to work toward—the album that was scheduled for 2005 with Island Def Jam. Work continued on the album, and the pieces seemed to be falling into place. She recorded music videos for the songs "Diamonds" and "Simple." The album, however, was doomed. Perry got the unexpected bad news that Island Def Jam was canceling her album. The explanation was that they simply did not know how to market Perry's music and her style.

Perry was stunned by the news and by some reactions to it. She recalled, "I had someone say to me that 'Psst, you should probably go home, because you're never gonna get signed again. You're pretty much damaged goods. And you should be in the defect aisle at Ross [discount stores]' … And I'm 20 at that point. I'm like, 'I'm defect[ive] goods already?'"[27]

Perry's album was not a total loss. Her song "Simple" was picked up for the film *The Sisterhood of the Traveling Pants* and was released on the movie soundtrack album in 2005.

## Repeated Challenges

In 2005, Perry was starting over again after the first record company that had signed her went bankrupt. Her chance to create a solo album with Island Def Jam had been crushed. Even her work with the Matrix had been abruptly discarded. She was still signed with Columbia as part of the Matrix project, so she and her manager, Bradford Cobb, convinced the company to let her record a solo album. However, Cobb revealed frustration with the entire relationship between Perry and Columbia. "Columbia was never really willing to embrace Katy's vision," he said. "They were not willing to let her drive. Here was this ambitious young woman with a clear picture of who she was and the willingness to work hard, and Columbia just wouldn't put her in the driver's seat."[28]

Work on Perry's album got underway despite differences of opinion. The album was due for release in 2006; however, Perry received more bad news. With the album nearly completed, Columbia decided to cancel her contract and drop the album. Cobb was shocked by the decision. He said, "Eighty percent of the record was done, and Columbia decided not to finish it and dropped her. We got the masters back and then started looking for a new home."[29] By convincing Columbia to turn over Perry's recordings to her, Cobb planned to offer the songs to other record companies and finally see the album released.

Perry clearly felt that something was wrong at Columbia. She said, "They dropped me, OneRepublic, and Jonas Brothers, in a matter of weeks. But what do you expect? Old guys in suits—they weren't the ones who were going out to the clubs or coming to the shows."[30] Ballard again showed his support for Perry and his distrust of the industry. "Nobody at those labels got what she was about," he said. "She had talent, personality, humor, a sense of fashion. They didn't know what to do with it."[31]

The cancellation was nearly the end of Perry's struggle for a music career. She explained one of the many of the obstacles she faced during this time, which was "overcoming everybody saying 'it's not going to work,' because a lot of people wanted me to be like someone—whether that was a Kelly Clarkson or an Avril Lavigne—and I was like 'I want to be Katy Perry first,' and they didn't really understand that."[32]

When Perry had first moved to Los Angeles at age 17, she had promised herself that she would keep trying for a music career until she was 25 years old. She was 22 years old when Columbia dropped her from their roster. Time and opportunities were beginning to run out.

# Perry's Big Break

Unbeknownst to Perry, she had recently gained an important secret fan in the music industry. Chris Anokute was an Artist and Repertoire executive at Capitol Records. He was young, and he was looking for a new artist whom he could launch completely from scratch.

Anokute had been introduced to Angelica Cob-Baehler, a publicity executive at Columbia Records, at the 2006 Grammy Awards show. Knowing that Columbia was about to drop Perry, Cob-Baehler secretly felt that executives at her company were making a major mistake. She gave Anokute an important tip about the then-unknown artist: "She's a singer-songwriter. She's incredible. She used to be a Christian singer and Columbia doesn't really know what to do with her and they are about to drop her."[33]

Chris Anokute (right) was one of Katy Perry's earliest supporters when others failed to give her a chance.

Anokute asked to get copies of Perry's music and received a DVD and three of Perry's demo CDs.

Anokute recalled his reaction when he first reviewed Perry's work: "It was an independent low budget video of a song called 'Simple'—an early song she did with Glen Ballard. For some reason I thought, 'Oh my god, she is a superstar.' She reminded me of Alanis Morissette. I listened to two other songs on the demo. One was 'Waking Up in Vegas' and when I heard that I thought, this is a number one record!"[34]

Determined to see Perry's career launched, Anokute took the recordings to Jason Flom, his boss at Capitol

Records. Anokute did not hold back his enthusiasm. He told Flom, "I've found the next Avril Lavigne meets Alanis Morissette."[35] However, Flom was not enthusiastic about Perry and was not convinced that her material and her image would sell. He also knew that Perry had been dropped from two previous record labels. Flom refrained from offering a contract to Perry. Anokute, however, refused to give up. Every week, he visited Flom's office to prove that Perry was worth signing. Anokute pleaded with his boss: "Jason, we'll find the record, we'll develop her, we'll figure it out! There is something special about her, I know she is a star. Who cares that she was dropped?"[36]

Perry finally became appealing to Flom in early 2007. Anokute remembers the moment: "I don't know what happened but one Sunday almost seven weeks later, Jason emails me, 'It's great, what are we waiting for? Let's sign the girl.' So we ... offered her a deal."[37]

## Making Ends Meet

Meanwhile, Perry had still been working to find ways to support herself and get her music heard. She seized any opportunity for work and exposure. One instance included singing and appearing in the music video for Christian metal group P.O.D.'s song "Goodbye for Now" in 2006. Around this time, she was featured in two other music videos: Carbon Leaf's "Learn to Fly" in 2006 and Gym Class Heroes' "Cupid's Chokehold" in 2005. In 2007, she modeled and appeared in advertisements for Too Faced cosmetics.

Even though she was landing gigs, life in Los Angeles was not always easy or glamorous. Perry often had to borrow money, and her checks sometimes bounced, which means that the check could not be processed because there was not enough money in her account to pay the check. Her car was repossessed twice when she could not make the payments for her car loan. She was forced to work at jobs she disliked to pay her rent. One of those jobs was at a company called TAXI Music where she had to critique other artists' record demos. "All these people want to get found. It was like ... torture listening to the worst music

# **Setting** Records

The Recording Industry Association of America (RIAA) represents U.S. artists and record companies. In 1958, it set the standard for the gold award, a tool that measures the sales of a record. A gold award is presented after an album sells more than 500,000 copies.

Due to the growth of the music industry, more awards were created to recognize even greater sales. In 1976, the platinum award was created to honor album sales of 1 million copies. In 1984, the multi-platinum award was established to reward sales of 2 million or more copies.

Katy Perry's album *One of the Boys* has achieved the platinum award. A number of her singles have reached the gold, platinum, and multi-platinum levels, with "I Kissed a Girl" at five-time multi-platinum (5 million copies). "California Gurls" and "Hot n Cold" are both seven-time multi-platinum (7 million copies). In July 2015, her third album, *Teenage Dream,* achieved sales of 3 million copies, earning it a 3-time multi-platinum award. Perry's fourth album, *Prism*, was certified two-time multi-platinum.

Her singles "Roar" and "Dark Horse" reached diamond status (at least 10 million copies). Her single "Firework" from *Teenage Dream* also became a diamond song.

As of 2017, the singles "Chained to the Rhythm" and "Swish Swish" from her album *Witness* have been certified platinum and gold, respectively.

ever ... and I was so depressed," Perry said. "How can I give any hope to these people?"[38] Fortunately, one day, Jason Flom called and scheduled to meet Perry for coffee, and after that, she never went back to the office.

# Fifth Time Is the Charm

In a new deal set up by Flom, Perry signed a recording contract with Capitol Records. For the fifth time, Perry was ready to record and release an album. In early 2007, she began recording the album that would eventually become *One of the Boys*.

Flom met with Lukasz Gottwald, known as Dr. Luke in the music industry. Dr. Luke was a recognized talent as a songwriter, record producer, and music mixer. He had worked with Perry at Columbia, but that album had never been finished. Flom asked Dr. Luke to work with Perry in the studio again. They recorded "I Kissed a Girl" and "Hot n Cold." Perry then worked with songwriter Greg Wells to write "Ur So Gay" and "Mannequin." To round out the album, Perry's team selected the best six songs from the tracks she had recorded at Columbia.

To test out public reaction to Perry's music, Capitol Records released "Ur So Gay" in November 2007 as an online single. The song caught some attention and sold a few thousand copies. Capitol also shot a low-budget video for the song, which got a great response from fans. Since the single was not a success, however, the executives at Capitol became nervous. Perry's album seemed like a gamble to them; they were not convinced it would become a hit.

Meanwhile, Anokute struggled to persuade his company to launch the album. He looked for a way to prove that Perry's music

Katy Perry and Dr. Luke (left) found success after recording her hit songs "I Kissed a Girl" and "Hot n Cold."

# Name Change

After moving to Los Angeles, Katy Hudson thought her name might be confused with actress Kate Hudson. By 2004, she had decided to change her name to avoid identity trouble.

Kate Hudson is an actress who became popular in the late 1990s. She is the daughter of Goldie Hawn, who starred in 2017's *Snatched* with Amy Schumer.

Hudson is known for her bubbly personality and versatile acting abilities. Her acting talents range from comedy to suspense to dance and musical theater. She appeared in the movies *How to Lose a Guy in 10 Days* with Matthew McConaughey in 2003, *The Skeleton Key* in 2005, and *Bride Wars* and *Nine* in 2009. She also appeared in the TV series *Glee* in 2012 and 2013. In 2001, she was nominated for an Academy Award for Best Supporting Actress for the movie *Almost Famous*.

Katy Hudson changed her stage name to Katy Perry in order to avoid people confusing her with the actress Kate Hudson, shown here.

would be a success. Eventually, he found a coworker, Dennis Reese, who was also excited about Perry. Reese offered the single "I Kissed a Girl" to a number of radio stations. A Nashville radio station called The River was the first to take an interest

Katy Perry is shown here celebrating the successful release of *One of the Boys* at her record release party on June 17, 2008, in Los Angeles.

and play the song on May 6, 2008. After only three days, the station was flooded with phone calls. Listeners could not get enough of Perry's song.

Capitol Records was finally convinced that Perry's album would sell. On June 17, 2008, *One of the Boys* was released. Anokute felt that their hard work had finally paid off. He explained,

> A lot of people think it happened overnight but it didn't ... It took us 14 to 18 month[s] to get her out, develop it and convince people. It wasn't easy to get her signed. I ... spent a year convincing people. I even had her come to the office, and no matter if it were interns, assistants, media people, sales people, I would just have her play acoustic guitar and showcase her songs to anyone that would listen. I had nine people standing around in my small office watching her play. This internal buzz building was happening for a year.[39]

Sales of the album proved, finally, that Capitol was wise to launch Katy Perry. *One of the Boys* landed on the Billboard Top 200 chart, appearing in the 9th position during the first week of its release. Perry was four months away from her 24th birthday when *One of the Boys* went on sale. She fulfilled her dream ahead of her goal.

# Chapter Three

# Finding Success in the Mainstream

Katy Perry finally achieved success after the release of her second album *One of the Boys*. Her song "I Kissed a Girl" was played nonstop on pop radio, and fans could not get enough of it. She became one of the most popular singers in the summer of 2008.

Some people assumed Perry had hopped onto the music scene as an overnight success, but what they did not know was that she had four false starts when trying to release *One of the Boys*. This moment had been years in the making, her drive to succeed in the music business was apparent, and she showed no signs of stopping.

## Experimenting with Fashion

As Perry gained recognition for her music, she was also being put in the spotlight by the media for her fashion style choices. Upon arriving in Hollywood, she discovered an endless array of fashions—some flattering, and some off-putting. In photos of Perry since 2002, her experimentation with style is visible. She can be seen in black rock-star-style leather, grunge outfits with torn jeans and loose tops, satin tops with pants or skirts, Bohemian combinations, and denim. She also appeared in outfits that seemed to be her own attempts to break the fashion rules—mixes of denim, florals, lace, leather, and boots. For one publicity photo, she copied Madonna's look from the 1980s—a strapless top, fishnet gloves, many long pearl necklaces, a stack of bangle bracelets, and heavy eyeliner. During this time, Perry also experimented with the image of a tough, attitude-wielding rocker with spiky hair.

Over the years, Perry eventually discovered her true sense of style. In 2006, her look shifted toward vintage feminine styles from the 1940s and 1950s. She wore dresses more often, especially the type with a fitted bodice (the part of a dress from the neck to the waist, excluding the sleeves) and full skirt that was popular in the 1950s. Her color choices also shifted away from neutrals, black, and denim to bright pastels, jewel tones, and bold colors. By 2007, she showed a taste for sequins.

Fashion critics were curious about Perry's broad range of tastes, especially considering her conservative background. Perry, however, believed that fashion had always been a part of her. She explained,

Katy Perry wore a vintage style outfit to the MTV Europe Music Awards in 2011.

*From an early age I've always loved the idea of surprising people with my outfits. I change from day to day. On a Monday I could be a Betty Boop figure. On a Tuesday I'll be Uma Thurman in* Pulp Fiction. *On a Wednesday I could be wearing [black] rubber. The next day I'll look like the innocent girl next door. Then there are days when … I'll dress normally in jeans and T-shirt. When I pop down [to] the grocery store … I leave all my glittery costumes at home. Most of the time I welcome attention, but there are days when I need to keep a healthy distance from it.*[40]

In 2008, Perry's fashion style developed focus. Of all the styles she tested over the years, one look emerged as her favorite. The style that made the biggest impact on her and would come to define her was that of the pinup girl.

## Finding Her Style

Pinup girls were young women who posed for advertisements during the 1940s and 1950s. The posters were generally of the women wearing shorts or skirts with a cropped top, and their hair and makeup were always perfectly styled. Long, wavy hair, pale skin, and bright red lipstick completed the signature look.

When Katy Perry discovered this style, she was hooked. She integrated the style into her own fashions, makeup, and hairstyles. She changed her hair color from a sun-streaked light brown to a dark chocolate brown and grew it longer to achieve the curls and waves that defined the style. Perry also kept her makeup very pale, with the exception of bright red lipstick.

Perry's clothing stood out as the strongest element of her style. In many of her concerts and public appearances, she chose outfits inspired by the styles of the 1950s. If any doubt remained about her love of this style, however, her album covers erased them.

The cover of Perry's album *One of the Boys* shows her reclining on a lounge chair, with a fringed pink blanket draping the chair. Perry wears high-waisted blue shorts and a 1950s-style top in red and white. A wide-brimmed blue sun hat, red sandals, and red-and-white bangle bracelets complete the look. Perry's lounge chair lies in an idealized backyard with a white picket fence, a thick green lawn, numerous colorful flowers, and a plastic pink flamingo lawn ornament. A 1950s pink record player stands nearby to complete the image.

The interior of the album booklet continues Perry's theme. Two more photos show her relaxing as if on a summer afternoon—on a lounge chair and in a kiddie pool. The back cover of the booklet features a close-up photo of Perry in a 1950s-style shirt with plastic cherries in her hair.

The album's booklet had been carefully planned. Perry and her team knew that Perry's image, as well as her music, would affect the rest of her career. Since her goal was to become a pop princess, she chose a style that she loved and that would allow her to explore her creativity. The result was a feminine, polished look that incorporated humor.

*One of the Boys* marked the beginning of a trend in Perry's style. Many of her outfits began to feature artificial fruit as props, jewelry, and costume elements. One of her most famous fruit-themed appearances was at the 2009 Grammy Awards show, where she performed in a dress decorated with sequined artificial fruit. She earned comparisons to Carmen Miranda, the singer from the 1940s and 1950s who wore costumes and elaborate headpieces that included huge flowers, baskets of fruit, and entire bunches of bananas. Perry said,

Katy Perry wore a dress with fake fruit attached to it during her performance at the 2009 Grammy Awards at the Staples Center in Los Angeles.

> *I've always been obsessed with fruit, so a lot of my costumes have featured things like strawberry hair clips and watermelon earrings. … At the Japanese MTV Video Awards I wore a leotard embroidered with pieces of sushi. People either look at me and share my enjoyment or else they vote for me in Worst Dressed Women lists.*[41]

Perry's unique look drew attention and blended perfectly with her musical style. She fueled headlines and news reports all across the country. Not only had her album launched, her career had launched, too.

## Endless Cameos

The entertainment business was also taking notice of newcomer Katy Perry. Almost out of nowhere, her schedule began to fill rapidly with projects and appearances. She filmed an episode of the cable TV series *Wildfire* in which she portrayed a club singer. Singing her own song on the show helped to stir interest in her music. Perry also appeared on an episode of the daytime drama *The Young and the Restless*. The program often featured new artists as a way of giving them exposure. Perry's appearance fell on June 12, 2008, less than a week before the release of her album. In the episode, Perry played herself. The scene depicted Perry posing for a photo shoot for a fictitious magazine. The glamour of the scene appealed to her feminine side.

Perry's music was also suddenly in demand. Her song "Fingerprints" was picked up to be part of the soundtrack for the 2008 movie *Baby Mama*. The group 3OH!3 also asked Perry to share vocals on their new song called "Starstrukk."

## Vans Warped Tour

One of Perry's steps on her journey to break out on the music scene was her appearance on the 2008 Vans Warped Tour. She had been invited on the tour the previous fall, while production on her album was still ongoing. A nationwide marathon, the Vans Warped Tour for 2008 consisted of 47 concerts sponsored by the shoe manufacturer Vans. Musical acts were accompanied in almost every city by an amateur skateboarding competition and a battle-of-the-bands contest for unsigned bands. The tour ran from June 20 to August 17. Perry was up to the challenge and was inspired by one of her idols. She explained, "Warped is going to be grueling and hot, but I'm ready to survive it—even without showers. Gwen Stefani did the tour back in 2000 with No Doubt and she looked fabulous hopping around on stage in her little polka-dotted dresses. I'm so channeling that."[42]

Perry, who wore colorful costumes, was an unusual addition to the Warped Tour. Since its beginnings in 1995, the tour has typically consisted of rock bands that are on the verge of launching

Katy Perry received positive reviews for her performances on the Vans Warped Tour in 2008.

their careers. In the tour's early years, the majority of bands were punk, but hip-hop and heavy metal bands were steadily added. The vast majority of musicians have been male. Fans of the tour are mostly people with a taste for alternative music and extreme sports.

In 2008, the tour included Paramore, 3OH!3, Gym Class Heroes, and others—a total of nearly 100 bands. The musicians at Warped Tour were generally split between three stages, with bands sometimes playing at the same time on different stages to accommodate the number of acts scheduled to perform. Perry was one of only a few female artists on the tour in 2008.

Perry received several good reviews for her performances on the tour. She was credited with having high energy and a playful and fun style. Some critics were surprised to discover that Perry was an excellent singer in a live setting. The *New York Times* wrote of a show at Nassau Coliseum in East Garden City, New York:

> *The final set of the day belonged to Katy Perry, an anomaly on this tour for several reasons: She is a woman; she is a pop singer; and she has a song, "I Kissed a Girl," which has spent the last month atop the* Billboard *singles chart. But in spite of a teal top and matching shorts, and perfect hair, she played to the scene, rolling around the stage like a rock star, and leading her band in heavier, more guitar-driven arrangements of her songs. By the time she closed with her big hit, boys were singing along, and dozens of girls were crowd-surfing.*[43]

## Dating Within the Music Industry

The Vans Warped Tour was exhausting and lacked luxuries.

# Pop Music Icon

Katy Perry has previously named singer Gwen Stefani as one of her fashion idols and pop music role models. Both have a taste for vintage fashion, makeup, and jewelry, and are recognized for their bold, unique styles. They often blend fun and whimsical elements into their costumes and performances.

Stefani was the lead singer of the band No Doubt. In 2002, the band took a break from performing so its members could spend time with family and recharge their creative energy. Since that time, Stefani has produced four solo albums: *Love. Angel. Music. Baby.* in 2004, *The Sweet Escape* in 2006, *This Is What the Truth Feels Like* in 2016, and *You Make It Feel Like Christmas* in 2017. The band reunited in 2010 and began to write songs for their sixth studio album, *Push and Shove*, which was released in 2012.

Stefani has long been considered a fashion icon as well as a performer. Her fashion choices range from

Performers lived on tour buses in the heat of summer and rarely had a day off from performing. During a performance in Maryland, Perry's shoes melted while they were on her feet. Perry told an interviewer that the majority of her dinners consisted of microwaved macaroni and cheese. Describing the grueling experience, Perry said,

> [Warped Tour] was one of the hardest things I've ever done because it was literally show after show after show, no showers ... we were all crammed into this bus and it was hot ... but I really held my own and I learned how to keep the attention of an audience ... and I learned the art of connecting with my audience.[44]

track pants and Doc Marten shoes to glamorous designer outfits. She is also known for a variety of themed costumes for her videos and TV appearances. Stefani's signature look is her platinum blonde hair, pale complexion, and bright red lipstick. Like Perry, she finds inspiration in vintage styles and in old movies and musicals such as *Rear Window* and *The Sound of Music*. Her own fashion idols are Marilyn Monroe, Grace Kelly, Jean Harlow, and Sophia Loren.

Gwen Stefani is constantly experimenting with combining different fashion styles, such as pinup, sporty, punk, and glamorous, among many others.

However, one thing that made the living conditions much more bearable for Perry was the presence of her then-boyfriend Travis McCoy of the band Gym Class Heroes. At the beginning of the Vans Warped Tour, Perry and McCoy had become a serious couple. McCoy gave Perry a ring with a diamond as a special gift and explained it was a promise ring—a symbol that they were committed to each other but without the significance of an engagement ring. McCoy also wore a promise ring that was silver and had the name "Katy" inscribed on it.

By the end of 2008, however, the relationship between McCoy and Perry had changed completely. The couple announced that they had broken up. Specific reasons were not given publicly, and Perry continued to make public appearances and greet the world with her usual energy.

# Enduring the Critics

By the end of September 2008, *One of the Boys* had sold 500,000 copies, earning Perry a gold record award.

High record sales are always a sign of success for a musician, but acceptance often depends on another aspect of the music business: reviews from music critics. Responses to Perry were mixed. Some critics praised her creativity and unique sound. Her voice and singing style received mostly positive comments. Reviewer Lizzie Ennever of the BBC, for example, gave *One of the Boys* a nod of approval. Ennever wrote,

> She manages to convey her emotions with a pretty varied and impressive vocal range. She's got a sound that's kind of Cerys Matthews crossed with Avril Lavigne, but there's a modern … tinge, which keeps One Of The Boys sounding fresh and funky …
>
> In general, this record is surprising—and in a good way … She has a wide variety of sounds and it'll be interesting to see where she goes with the follow-up.[45]

Perry's songs and lyrics caused some confusion among other critics, however. Many questioned whether Perry would be capable of putting out a follow-up album or if all her creative energy had been used up. Some called "I Kissed a Girl" a novelty song—a song with a catchy melody but silly lyrics without meaning. Others called her lyrics tasteless or empty. Some felt that she would never be able to build a career on novelty songs and lyrics that were fluff without deeper meaning. Reviewer Stacey Anderson from *Spin* magazine was one critic with nothing good to say about the album. Anderson gave *One of the Boys* a 3 on a scale of 1 to 10. She wrote that the album had "no discernible message, just a bleating electroclash soundtrack." The reviewer singled out the song "Ur So Gay" by describing it as "a brassy, hiccupping beat, it's momentarily novel, but soon the song wears … thin."[46] Similarly, reviewer Genevieve Koski gave Perry's album a grade of D-. She complained that the album lacked substance and wrote, "While undeniably catchy, the hyper-produced songs have a familiar radio-ready quality that becomes infuriatingly mind-numbing over time, and Perry's vocals sound like a less-soulful Kelly Clarkson at best."[47]

Predictions for Perry were also mixed. Some critics speculated that she would enjoy a long career. One critic at *Billboard* magazine felt that she had produced an entire album of hit songs; a reviewer from the website MusicOMH called her album "sparky and accomplished."[48] Others, however, did not understand the appeal. Another reviewer dismissed her album as being overstuffed with instrumental pop gimmicks and not enough true writing talent. He wrote, "Her songs are hooky as all get-out, but they're also packed to the gills with clichés, many of them about how she wants to 'break the mold' ... This is annoying at first ... but it ultimately winds up just being boring."[49]

Whether the critiques were positive or negative, one thing was clear: Perry had been noticed. As 2008 came to a close, her album and singles were selling at a fast pace.

## Katy's First Tour

After finishing the Vans Warped Tour and breaking up with her boyfriend at the end of 2008, January 2009 brought new opportunities for Perry. Her next major career event was upon her: On January 23, 2009, her worldwide concert tour celebrating *One of the Boys* began in Seattle, Washington. Perry's experiences on past tours helped prepare her for a major tour of her own.

Perry's new tour, called *Hello Katy*, sold out around the world. It lasted nearly a year and took her across the United States and to various locales in Asia, Europe, and Australia. It began with visits to nine cities on the West Coast and then jumped across the Atlantic Ocean to Germany. The concerts continued in 11 European cities, including London and Paris. In mid-March, she returned to the United States and played in 16 more cities, beginning in Houston, Texas, and zigzagging north through the Midwest, east to New York and Washington, D.C., and south again to Florida. In late May, she performed four shows in Japan. Then, after a trip to the Netherlands, she performed 21 more concerts across Europe. Perry was not nearly finished. The tour continued through June, July, and August, traveling back to North America, then on to Australia, and

Katy Perry always makes an effort to connect with her fans in the crowd while performing onstage.

back to Europe and North America. In November, the tour finally concluded.

From past experiences, Perry knew the concerts would be more work than glamour. "I knew it would be hard work, but it is really a lot of hard work," she said. "Lots of people who have pretty normal jobs have the weekends off, nights off, not for me. I have no weekends, and on top of that you can't get sick, you're going to all kinds of different countries." Despite the challenges, Perry was grateful for her opportunities, as she explained: "There's no complaining ever, I'm not complaining at all ... I know there are, like, 500 girls behind me that want it more than I do or as much as I do."[50]

Reviews of the concerts were generally good. British reviewer Alice Fisher from the newspaper the *Observer* credited Perry's high energy, creativity, and humor and wrote, "Perry's real magic comes from what so many singers lack: her personality."[51] Perry got especially high marks for her unique ability to surpass typical pop star performers who are often similar and easily forgotten.

By the end of her world tour, Perry's career seemed solid. Her album had received a platinum award in February 2009 after selling 1 million copies. Her singles were achieving multi-platinum status, yet she was still considered a new artist, with only one major album to her credit. The time had come for Perry to release another album. Fans, industry observers, and critics all watched to see if her career would explode like a firework or merely fizzle.

# Chapter Four

# Riding the Fame Wave

**N**ow that Perry had adjusted to the idea of being famous, she started to look forward to the next phases of her life as a musician, which meant putting out another album. The release of *One of the Boys* was meant to help her gain exposure as an artist. After the success of this album, she finally had a following she hoped would stay loyal and stick with her when she released her next album.

## The Dreaded Follow-Up Album

In the music industry, an artist's second album, commonly called the sophomore album, is considered a test and a turning point. Often, artists release a first album that has great success. Their combination of talent, song choices, and image make a positive impact on the public. The true test of a musician's talent and potential, however, is often measured by their second album. In some cases, the second album marks the end of a career because it does not live up to the creativity of the first album. Sometimes, an appearance in a popular movie or a reality TV show drives sales of the first album, but the artist's talent is limited and does not support another album. In other cases, a follow-up album sells poorly because it comes too long after the first album, and fans forget about an artist or their taste in music has changed. The challenge of a second album is to create a music offering that is better than the first and to show that the first album had not simply been a stroke of luck.

In Perry's case, her first album under the name Katy Perry was actually considered her second album, since she had first released a Christian album in 2001. For Perry, it was her third release (second under the name Katy Perry) that would serve as her mainstream follow-up. This album needed to prove to her record company that she could continue to write hit songs and sell albums. With this upcoming album she was also free to branch out into different styles and themes. However, in the background was the pressure that came with a follow-up album after achieving such success with a previous album. Perry and her team knew that her next album needed to exceed the quality of *One of the Boys* and also make a new statement about Perry and her talent.

Chris Anokute was again Perry's representative at Capitol Records. He carefully considered the direction of Perry's new album. Anokute recalled,

> We wanted to try something different, more rhythmic on the [dance floor] without losing who Katy Perry was. So I introduced her to new producers like Tricky Stewart, Stargate and Rodney Jerkins. It was cool for her because she'd never worked with an urban producer. But I thought it would give her a different kind of edge, especially since she's a singer songwriter who brings the main ideas to the table when collaborating with producers.[52]

Anokute wanted to make sure that Perry continued to grow as an artist. He knew that she needed to sound a bit more mature to be taken seriously. By arranging collaborations with new artists and producers of varying tastes and styles, Perry learned how to integrate new sounds and techniques. As she expanded her musical skills and depth, she learned to demonstrate a solid foundation and stretch her creativity.

Perry knew she wanted her second album, *Teenage Dream*, to get people out of their seats. "When I was touring I wanted people to be able to dance more, so I wrote an album that made

people move, yet didn't sacrifice the story substance that I had on the last album,"[53] she said. In a video on her website, Perry described her different visions for the two albums and explained that she tried to make the second album more mature than the first. "The last record to me was a little bit more Betty Boop," she said. "It was very cutesy. And this record is a little bit more … [Roy] Lichtenstein 90s pop art … It's still colorful but in a different way. And it's funny … on the first record I had this obsession with, like, fruit and now it's turned into, like, candy and like, baked goods."[54]

Katy Perry incorporated enlarged candy and baked goods props into her stage sets when performing songs from *Teenage Dream*.

## Making Hit Songs

Perry's biggest hits on *Teenage Dream*, "Teenage Dream" and "California Gurls," were the last songs to be added to the record. Anokute remembers the birth of Perry's idea for "California Gurls." Although her album was nearly finished, she sent him a late-night text message insisting that she needed to write one more song. After thinking about the song "Empire State of Mind" by JAY-Z and Alicia Keys, which praised New York City, Perry was inspired to write a song about California.

Anokute said, "I heard the demo and I was floored. She had a vision for Snoop [Dogg] to guest on the record. I was close to his camp, so I contacted his manager Ted Chung that same day and [said], 'I got a smash for Snoop [and] Katy Perry. It's called 'California Gurls' and it will bring him back to Top 40 radio."[55]

On his next visit to Los Angeles, Snoop Dogg listened to the song and recorded his contributions to the record. Anokute said it was a huge moment: "He listens to 'California Gurls' [with just Perry's

# Vintage Shopping

Katy Perry has a hobby that few people know about: rummaging for secondhand treasures at garage sales and thrift shops. Considering her taste for vintage clothes and styles, this love of tag sales is not surprising. As she told an interviewer in 2009,

*From the age of eight, my dad would wake me up early on a Saturday morning and we'd go to garage sales ... I'd find a purple glass doorknob from the Twenties and it would be going for a song [that is, very inexpensive]. I have a good eye. I'm not looking to make any huge profits. I'm just drawn to old, well-made stuff that has its own personality. Wherever I am in the world, you can usually find me rummaging through antique shops. Nothing beats the thrill of wandering into a shop in the middle of Australia and picking up the vintage handbag of my dreams for a few dollars.*[1]

1. Quoted in Jon Wilde, "I'm a Natural-Born Glamour Ninja—and I Like It: Katy Perry on Her Unique Style," *Mail Online*, July 21, 2009. www.dailymail.co.uk/home/moslive/article-1198292/Im-natural-born-glamour-ninja--I-like-Katy-Perry.html.

Katy Perry enjoys experimenting with her style and sometimes incorporates vintage elements into her outfits.

vocals] and then … 30 minutes later we're listening to 'California Gurls' featuring Snoop!"[56] Anokute gave Perry full credit for the

After Katy Perry and Snoop Dogg, both originally from California, released the song "California Gurls," it was immediately well-received by her fans.

vision of the song and told an interviewer that she had incredible instincts.

The other latecomer to Perry's album was the song "Teenage Dream." She described it as one of her songs in which she pours out all of her feelings. At different times, Perry had expressed how important it was for her to connect with her audience emotionally. This song had an especially strong emotional charge for her, as she explained: "It's about that feeling that I think so many people relate to ... when they get to their 20s and 30s and remember being a teenager and putting all or nothing into a relationship, and usually getting hurt, but it was such an amazing feeling—so pure and lovely and raw."[57]

Perry was continuously aware of what was at stake with her second album. Even though she had a strong fan base and had made it past the hurdle of her breakthrough album, she could not afford to be lazy. "How many times do you see people slump on their sophomore record?" she told a reporter for the *Guardian*. "Nine out of 10."[58]

## Mixed Reviews

In May 2010, the single "California Gurls" was leaked to radio stations. The day after it was leaked, it was the number one song in America downloaded from iTunes. "California Gurls" became the theme song of the summer, with its catchy dance beat and lyrics that tapped into a summery pulse. Three months passed before the album *Teenage Dream* was released, with the album going on sale on August 24, 2010. In the first week, it sold 192,000 copies and appeared in the number one position on the Billboard Top 200 chart.

Despite its impressive sales, reviews of *Teenage Dream*, like the ones for *One of the Boys*, were mixed. Reviewer Kitty Empire from the British publication the *Observer* thought Perry's songs lacked the wit and humor of *One of the Boys* and that some of the songs, such as "E.T.," did not match Perry's image. She also complained that Perry's attempt at meaningful lyrics was merely a string of clichés. Empire noted, "Perry's second album is a hard-nosed pop product with little of the humour or wit expressed so fluently by her wardrobe," and she referred to "California Gurls" as "pretty lame."[59] Chris Richards of the *Washington Post* could not deny the appeal and catchiness of "California Gurls" but dismissed her other songs as weak, and he wrote that "the hooks are consistently grabby, but even Perry's catchiest refrains quickly start to [annoy] if you actually pay attention to the words."[60]

The *Los Angeles Times* gave Perry credit for creativity and building an image. It also praised her ability to succeed in different musical styles. The paper's review complained, though, that the album seemed focused on consumerism and was designed more like a series of advertisements than a truly artistic album.

Rob Sheffield of *Rolling Stone* magazine, on the other hand, gave the album credit for clever songwriting and called it a winner. He wrote, "It's miles ahead of Perry's breakthrough disc,

Katy Perry's "Firework" became one of her most well-respected songs with its positive and hopeful message.

*One of the Boys*, with … clever songwriting."[61]

Some of the most positive responses to Perry's album came in reaction to her song "Firework." The lyrics were recognized as speaking to anyone who feels down on their luck or in a bad situation. The chorus pushes the listener to keep trying, face difficult problems, and make an impact in the world. The song was praised for its encouraging message and became a frequent request at Perry's public appearances. "Firework" became an anthem for perseverance and hard work and was included on many television shows and in advertisements.

## Giving Back to Her Fans

As Perry gained confidence in her status as a performer, she found new ways to embrace her fame. She discovered that she had opportunities both to give back to her fans and use her talents to benefit others.

Inspired by her own song, Perry launched a "Firework" contest on her website in 2010. She asked fans to tell her about someone in their lives whom they considered a firework—a person who was inspirational or influential. Fans were asked to record a video and post it to YouTube. Six entries were selected as finalists, and the videos were posted to Perry's website. In January 2011, college student Cory Woodard was named the grand-prize winner. He named his mother as his firework for always inspiring and encouraging him even though he was confined to a wheelchair. He was awarded a trip along with three guests to one of Perry's future concerts in London, England. The contest generated many uplifting stories and brought a new depth to Perry's website.

Perry took advantage of an opportunity to entertain and honor members of the American military in December 2010. The event was filmed at the Marine Corps Air Station Miramar in San Diego, California. The concert, sponsored by VH1, was called *USO Presents: VH1 Divas Salute the Troops* and included Nicki Minaj, Sugarland, Keri Hilson, Grace Potter, and other performers. The lineup included Perry in a camouflage dress performing "Girls Just Wanna Have Fun" with Nicki Minaj; her rendition of "Firework" in a full-length, red sequined gown; as well as two other

## Singer Secrets

Perry once shared a secret about her recording style with an interviewer. "One of the unique things about me recording is that I like to put down the vocal track with all the lights off in the studio. If I remember the lyrics, I don't want anything to get in the way. I want to be a voice in the darkness."[1] Although Perry enjoys studio sessions because she can take her time with the music, she prefers to play live because of the chance it offers to interact with the audience and feed off of their energy.

1. Quoted in Mike Burr, "Katy Perry: Interview," *Prefix*, February 6, 2008. www.prefixmag.com/features/interview/17027/.

appearances. Toward the end of the show, she told her audience, "Be careful out there during the holidays," and understanding their separation from loved ones, added, "I just hope everybody can find a great Christmas and be blessed."[62] Perry received a number of complimentary reviews for her performances.

Several causes also have Katy Perry as a supporter, including breast cancer awareness, an AIDS initiative concert sponsored by musician Bono, other AIDS groups, and an effort by Gibson Guitars to support Nashville flood relief. She has also appeared in several benefit concerts in the United States, Canada, and Europe. These and other charitable contributions came as a result of Perry's newfound fame. As career opportunities kept pouring in for Perry, she continued to integrate helping others into her hard-earned success.

# Chapter **Five**

# Love, Loss, and Inspiration

**K**aty Perry's successful albums got people talking, and her videos and style kept them interested. This combination made her irresistible for appearances on television, in movies, on award shows, and in concert. On the heels of her popular albums, Perry was a virtual domino effect of activity, moving from one appearance to another in a seemingly endless stream. Her traveling, public appearances, and whirlwind romance throughout 2009 and 2010 must have truly felt like a teenage dream come true.

## *Whirlwind Romance*

Perry's fame brought her many new experiences, but one particular invitation permanently impacted her life. During the summer of 2009, Perry was invited to make a cameo appearance in the movie *Get Him to the Greek*. She was slated to act in a scene with the movie's star, Russell Brand, who played an out-of-control British rock star preparing to make a comeback. Despite Brand's reputation, Perry described him as "really gentle in person and just had this vibe about him that was captivating."[63] Both Perry and Brand enjoyed the scene and were happy with the results, but it was eventually cut from the movie.

Perry crossed paths with Brand again in September at the

Katy Perry and Russell Brand first met on the movie set of *Get Him to the Greek*.

MTV 2009 Video Music Awards show at Radio City Music Hall in New York City. Perry attended the awards show as a nominee for Best Female Video for her song "Hot n Cold." Brand was hosting the Video Music Awards for the second year in a row, and he made a dramatic, rock-star-style entrance onto the stage amid fireworks and special effects. He was accompanied by Katy Perry and guitarist Joe Perry of Aerosmith. Together, they sang Queen's "We Will Rock You." Brand kept the audience laughing with a stream of jokes.

Perry described her encounter with Brand as somewhat flirtatious. "I really gave him a run for his money," she told an interviewer for *Seventeen* magazine. "I was just hamming it up with him, and we were very comically competitive, but we also had some nice conversations."[64] The pair later went out to dinner together.

Soon after, Perry found herself in a predicament. She and a friend had plans to vacation in Thailand, but her friend became sick and had to back out. Perry and Brand had been communicating through email, and Brand offered to go on the trip with her when he heard the news about her friend. Perry thought the plan was crazy, but they met at the airport and jetted to Thailand together. That trip, which Perry described as their "second date," led to other vacations in Paris and London, and the pair soon revealed they were dating.

When their attraction turned to love, Perry decided to reveal her feelings to Brand in her typically flamboyant way. She hired a skywriter to spell out "I Love You" above his home. The experience turned out to be somewhat nerve-racking for Perry, as she

# The Life of Russell Brand

Russell Brand is a British actor and comedian. As a performer, he is known for his endless energy and his willingness to try almost anything. In public, his style appears to be a cross between rock star and 19th-century poet, blending black jeans, ruffled shirts, jackets, leather, and heavy jewelry. He is also famous for his long, unruly hair. In addition, Brand is known to some for his battle with drug and alcohol addiction and for dating many women.

Brand has appeared in several movies. He played Adam Sandler's wacky best friend in the 2008 film *Bedtime Stories*. Also in 2008, he appeared as the character Aldous Snow in the movie *Forgetting Sarah Marshall* and later played the lead role in the 2010 film *Get Him to the Greek*. In 2011, he played the title character in the remake of the romantic comedy *Arthur*. Brand has also done voice actor work on the animated films *Despicable Me, Hop,* and *Despicable Me 2*.

Russell Brand is a British actor, comedian, radio host, and author. He has been featured in a number of films.

explained: "He hadn't told me he loved me yet, but I was just gonna take a chance because I could feel it … And thank God he told me he loved me that morning. I didn't really even say it back because I wanted to save it. We walked out to the balcony of his house, and I said, 'Look up.'"[65]

## An Extravagant Proposal

The romance between Perry and Brand continued to sizzle. When Perry told Brand she loved Indian culture, he arranged for them to go to India as a Christmas gift. Together, they enjoyed traditional tourist sites such as the Taj Mahal, and Perry had her hand painted with a henna tattoo. The highlight of the trip was on New Year's Eve in Jaipur, when Brand surprised Perry with an engagement ring. Perry accepted his proposal happily, and the news was made public by their agents on January 6, 2010.

Perry's ring became the focus of great attention. While in Delhi, Brand had secretly met with jewelry designer Hanut Singh, who had been recommended by friends. Singh showed Brand some of his favorite designs as well as a rare Golconda diamond from India—diamonds that have a reputation as the purest stones in the world. Brand made up his mind easily. A few weeks later, Perry's ring was sought after by photographers once news of the engagement went public.

## Wedding Bells

Throughout 2010, Perry's and Brand's public appearances were sweet, authentic, and even funny. When asked why Perry was so special on the television show *The View*, for example, Brand said, "As soon as I met her, she was a long way away, maybe like forty yards away, she threw a bottle right across the room and hit me on the head and at first I thought, a woman with an arm like that could be useful in a marriage, for defense purposes." He admitted that his head hurt after getting hit and that people around him laughed, but he was intrigued. He expressed his sentiments about her by saying, "I want to take care of her and I love her."[66]

By May 2010, reports circulated that their wedding would take place sometime in October. Later news revealed it would be held in India. When the couple was spotted boarding a plane to India on October 20, the entertainment media started scrambling for coverage. Perry, however, begged for privacy on her Twitter page: "Greatest gift u can give us is respect & ♥ during this private X. No use wasting ur X w/ STOLEN or FALSE info. Thnku for this."[67] In other words, Perry was asking for respect during this private time and asked for reporters to not waste their own time by reporting false information.

## Top Secret Wedding

A few days later, Perry's and Brand's representatives confirmed that the couple had gotten married on October 23, 2010, in the countryside of northern India. A Christian minister, a longtime friend of Perry's parents, performed the ceremony. Only invited guests—family and friends—were in attendance. Various reports estimated there were between 70 and 100 guests.

A number of colorful rumors followed the wedding. One claimed that Brand's wedding gift to his new wife was a tiger. This was false; tigers are protected animals in India and cannot be bought or sold. Some of the gossip also described the wedding festivities as going on for a full week, yet the bride and groom were in the country for only five days.

Accurate details about the wedding trickled forth in the weeks following the ceremony. Brand, Perry, and their guests stayed at a resort near Ranthambore National Park, a wildlife sanctuary known for its tiger population, not far from Jaipur. Guests were treated to traditional Indian music, acrobats, jugglers, and safari trips. On the day of the wedding, the trees lining the entrance to the sanctuary were covered in white lights.

Photos of the bride and groom were absent in the media. Reporters spent a great amount of time guessing the details of the wedding, especially Perry's wedding gown. To the disappointment of fans and the media, the couple never released any wedding photos to the public. Two days after their wedding, Perry and Brand flew to the Maldives for their honeymoon—and to celebrate Perry's 26th birthday the same day.

# **Cartoon** Fun

During the summer of 2010, Perry recorded the voice of Smurfette for a new movie version of *The Smurfs*, which was released in July 2011. Perry found her role to be especially funny, since she had not been allowed to watch the cartoon as a child. "I've never seen an episode [of 'The Smurfs'] because my parents wouldn't let me," she explained. "My mom thought that Smurfette was [not a good role model] ... And now I showed her. I called her up and was like, 'Guess what, Mom: I'm Smurfette!'"[1]

Then, in December 2010, Perry was featured in the holiday special for the animated series *The Simpsons*. She provided her voice for the animated scenes and, in a first for the show, played in live action scenes with puppet versions of the Simpson family.

Perry later reprised her role as Smurfette in *The Smurfs 2*, which was released in July 2013. Other returning voice actors from the first film included Hank Azaria, Neil Patrick Harris, Jayma Mays, and George Lopez.

1. Quoted in James Montgomery, "Katy Perry Says She Wasn't Allowed to Watch 'The Smurfs' Growing Up," MTV.com, June 7, 2010. www.mtv.com/news/articles/1640953/katy-perry-wasnt-allowed-watch-smurfs-growing-up.jhtml.

# California Dreams *Tour*

After enjoying a few months together as newlyweds, Perry and Brand were forced to endure long stretches of separation due to Perry embarking on a massive worldwide tour in support of her second album, *Teenage Dream*. The *California Dreams* tour kicked off in Lisbon, Portugal, on February 20, 2011, and continued throughout Europe until the first week of April. After a break of about two weeks, the tour continued in Australia and New Zealand until May 15. Perry then jetted to Japan for a few concerts, finishing on May 26. Next, she played an extensive list of shows in North America and Latin America from June 7 to September 27. The tour went through the United Kingdom in October and continued in Europe through the first week of November before returning to the United States for a few shows in the remainder of November. Finally, she performed in Indonesia and the Philippines in January 2012.

Throughout the course of this tour, Perry and Brand would take turns flying back and forth to one another to spend time with each other whenever Perry had a few days off in between tour dates. While they knew it would test their marriage, both parties were ready to take on the challenge. Speaking on her expectations of finding her true love, Perry said, "I thought to myself, 'When I find that person that's going to be my life partner, I won't ever have to choose [between the partner and my career]. They won't be threatened or have weird motives.'"[68]

Unfortunately, this grueling schedule began to take a toll on the couple's marriage. In her documentary and concert film, *Katy Perry: Part of Me*, which was released in July 2012, Perry becomes noticeably rundown and depressed while on tour after continuously performing night after night and being unable to see her husband. As her marriage began to unravel, Perry was determined to finish out her tour, despite the issues she faced in her personal life.

Katy Perry wore a variety of costumes that were colorful and elaborate on her *California Dreams* tour.

## Five Numbers Ones

In 2011, Perry became the first woman and second artist following Michael Jackson to have 5 of her songs from the same album reach number 1 on the Billboard Hot 100 chart. These songs from her third album *Teenage Dream* include "Last Friday Night (T.G.I.F.)," "California Gurls" (featuring Snoop Dogg), "Firework," "E.T." (featuring Kanye West), and the title track. In an exclusive statement to *Billboard*, she expressed her gratitude:

*Hitting No. 1 is always a great moment, but when it turns into a small piece of history, you're reminded of how many millions of people are connected to each other by even one tiny event ... Thank you to everyone who helped make this happen. Ever since I was 9 years old, singing into my hairbrush, I've dreamed very big dreams, but today is bigger than my dreams. What a nice first birthday present for "Teenage Dream"![1]*

## Trouble in Paradise

On New Year's Eve 2011, Brand sent Perry a text message asking for a divorce after just 14 months of marriage. The divorce was finalized in July 2012. The official cause of the split has never been revealed as of 2017. As Perry explained, "Nobody knows what really happened except the two people who are in it,"[69] referring to herself and Brand.

Brand also took it upon himself to discuss the demise of their marriage in his 2015 documentary *BRAND: A Second Coming*. In the film, Brand recalled his time with Perry, as photos of the former couple flash across the screen, describing it as, "I'm living this life of the very thing I detest. Vapid [uninteresting], vacuous [mindless] celebrity."[70] He also took it a step further and mocked

Michael Jackson first achieved the feat with his 1987 album *Bad* with his hit singles "I Can't Stop Loving You," "Bad," "The Way You Make Me Feel," "Man in the Mirror," and "Dirty Diana."

1. Quoted in Gary Trust, "Katy Perry Makes Hot 100 History: Ties Michael Jackson's Record," *Billboard*, August 17, 2011. www.billboard.com/articles/news/467879/katy-perry-makes-hot-100-history-ties-michael-jacksons-record.

Michael Jackson was one of the most iconic and successful music artists of his time and continues to be recognized as such by many of his fans and music critics.

Perry by showcasing his best impersonation of her accent.

Perry admits her world tour made it extremely difficult to maintain a stable relationship with Brand. However, she said she invited him to come visit her constantly and tried to come home to see him as much as she possibly could. While she was succeeding in her music career, her marriage was crumbling, but the effort she put in to try to save it was worth it, she said. "I have that same belief system with everything, from career to my life to my personal life, everything. And I will do everything it takes to not fail," she said. "And I did everything it took, but it still failed."[71]

In an intimate segment of *Katy Perry: Part of Me*, Perry is delayed from getting on stage in Brazil because she cannot stop crying; the cause of her sadness clearly was due to the distance between her and Brand, as she clutched a necklace he gave her for her birthday while sobbing. Her staff, approaching her in a sensitive fashion, asks her if she wants to cancel the show or go out there and do her best. Ultimately, after wiping her tears away and having her makeup done, she chooses to go ahead with the performance.

Looking back on their relationship, Perry said at first Brand seemed to be supportive of her goals, but somewhere along the way, their connection was lost. "At first when I met him he wanted an equal, and I think a lot of times strong men do want an equal, but then they get that equal and they're like, I can't handle the equalness," Perry told *Vogue*. "He didn't like the atmosphere of me being the boss on tour. So that was really hurtful, and it was very controlling, which was upsetting."[72]

## "Wide Awake"

Once Perry was able to process the shock of her divorce from Brand, she returned to the life she knew best—releasing music. In March 2012, she put out a reissue of *Teenage Dream* titled *Teenage Dream: The Complete Confection*. This reissue included all the songs from the original *Teenage Dream* album, an acoustic version of "The One That Got Away," three remixes, and two new singles: "Part of Me" and "Wide Awake." The reissue album peaked at number 7 on the Billboard Top 200 chart, while the lead single "Part of Me" debuted at number 1 and the second single "Wide Awake" debuted at number 2 on the Billboard Hot 100.

While Perry may have suffered a loss in her life after going through her divorce from Brand, she was gaining more and more recognition as a pop artist and finding her confidence in each new step she took. Her future appeared bright as she plotted her next album. She was ready to release music that expressed feelings and experiences that were more intimate and close to her. This album became her fourth release, *Prism*.

# Chapter Six

# Prismatic Epiphanies

As Perry recovered from the end of her marriage to Russell Brand, she had big plans for her next album. She had evolved so much since the start of her music career, and it was time for another evolution. With her fourth album, she wanted to give her fans a deeper look inside some of her most intimate emotions and experiences.

## Making of Prism

In June 2012, when Perry first opened up about her plans for *Prism*, she told *L'Uomo Vogue* the album "would be a much darker album than the previous one. It was inevitable, after what I went through."[73] However, after some time passed, the result was less dark than Perry had anticipated and more healing and uplifting.

While still on tour promoting *Teenage Dream*, she began recording snippets of ideas into a dictaphone on her iPhone. These snippets were then transcribed by Ngoc Hoang, a member of her team at Direct Management Group, and put in what she called a "treasure chest." It was not until November 2012 that she entered the studio and began working with longtime producers Greg Kurstin and Greg Wells.

# Giving Back

Katy Perry was named Goodwill Ambassador for UNICEF in December 2013 "with a special focus on encouraging young people in the agency's work to help improve the lives of the world's most vulnerable children and adolescents."[1]

"I believe young people have the power to change their own lives, with our help," Perry said after being named a Goodwill Ambassador. "I am honoured to join UNICEF as a Goodwill Ambassador, and committed to doing everything I can to help children and adolescents who come from such different backgrounds but want the same thing: a brighter future."[2]

After taking a trip with UNICEF to Madagascar, Africa, Perry became passionate about extending her outreach to children in need. In a UNICEF video, Perry spoke about how those in the United States and elsewhere can help those in other countries: "We have to look beyond our countries and help all the other children because they deserve it, too. And we need to raise a generation that has a different way of thinking. That has

After a humanitarian trip with UNICEF to Madagascar, Africa, Perry returned with an enlightened outlook and was ready to dive back into working on *Prism*. Eckhart Tolle, the author of the best-selling book *The Power of Now*, had also inspired her with a six-minute video. One of the lines that spoke to her was, "When you lose something, all your foundations crumble—but that also leaves a big hole that's open for something great to come through."[74] She had also begun practicing transcendental meditation and mindfulness therapy.

From there, she partnered up with longtime producer Lukasz

empathy and compassion so that they can have that with their children."[3]

In October 2013, Perry signed on for UNICEF's celebration of the International Day of the Girl Child to help support and inspire young girls to become empowered leaders. She also let them use her song "Roar" on the soundtrack for the celebration's PSA.

Katy Perry connected with the children and teenagers of Madagascar, Africa, as shown here. She believes all children should be able to have a bright future.

1. "Katy Perry is UNICEF's Newest Goodwill Ambassador," UNICEF, December 3, 2013. www.unicef.org/media/media_71241.html.

2. Quoted in "Katy Perry is UNICEF's Newest Goodwill Ambassador," UNICEF.

3. Quoted in "Katy Perry Talks Inspiration Behind "Unconditionally"/ UNICEF," YouTube video, 2:05, posted by UNICEF. December 9, 2013. www.youtube.com/watch?v=D_W8vFeTSZO.

"Dr. Luke" Gottwald, and songwriters Bonnie McKee and Henry Walter in Santa Barbara, California, for a month. Next, she traveled to Stockholm, Sweden, to work with Max Martin for a few weeks. In addition, she also worked with Benny Blanco, Jonatha Brooke, Stargate, Sia, Juicy J, Christian "Bloodshy" Karlsson, and Klas Åhlund of the Teddybears to fully develop her fourth album.

"I didn't want to do Teenage Dream 2.0," Perry said. "*Teenage Dream* was highly conceptual, super-pop art. 'PRISM' is more organic, au naturale, vulnerable and honest, but still has the same amount of fun."[75]

# Releasing New Music

The result of all the hard work put into *Prism* was an empowering lead single "Roar," which debuted in August 2013 and topped the Billboard Hot 100. In the music video for the song, Perry is seen surviving a plane crash and braving it out in the jungle alone after a tiger attacks the man she is with. In the beginning, she is afraid of all the frightening elements of the jungle, such as large spiders and crocodiles, but then by the end of the video, she is confidently swinging from a tree's vines and taming a tiger.

The second single released from *Prism*, "Unconditionally," was released on October 16, 2013, two days before the release of the full album. The track was inspired by her trip to Madagascar with UNICEF earlier in the year where she says she felt surrounded by "unconditional love:"

> *I saw all these children interacting with each other. There's so much love between them and their exchanges. There's so much compassion between them. And they don't have anything. They don't have any material possessions. They don't have any social status. It's an unconditional love. It's a non-judgmental love. So I was just really inspired by that kind of high-level of love that they're trading over there.*[76]

Following the release of *Prism* on October 18, 2013, the album topped the Billboard Top 200 with 286,000 copies sold in its first week. Overall, the album was primarily dance-inspired with hints of subtle dark elements, which she had originally planned to incorporate in a larger capacity on the album. The critiques of the album were mixed but generally positive. When *Billboard* reviewed the album, they only offered up compliments: "'PRISM' has its share of candy-colored fun, but also something else: more detail in its tempered shades. With a string of hit singles under her belt, Perry has aspired to create a multifaceted full-length and has consummately succeeded."[77]

While *Prism* received high recognition from some, it also generated hopeful, yet less praiseworthy reviews from other outlets,

# **John** Mayer

Singer-songwriter John Mayer and Katy Perry had an on-again, off-again relationship from 2012 to 2015. The couple released a duet in 2013 titled "Who You Love," which was included on Mayer's sixth album, *Paradise Valley*. Mayer's description of the song is, "I love you based on the fact that I've tried to run and I'm not running and I give up."[1]

Since parting ways with Perry in 2015, Mayer has used his experiences from the relationship and break-up to create some of the songs included on his seventh studio album, *The Search for Everything*, which was released on April 14, 2017. He admitted that Perry was his only long-term relationship for the last five or six years. "There were times when tears came out of me, and I went, OK, John, this is not about an on-again, off-again relationship. This is something more profound."[2] Mayer admitted the songs "Still Feel Like Your Man," "You're Gonna Live Forever in Me," and "Moving On and Getting Over" are about Perry, telling the *New York Times*, "Who else would I be thinking about?"[3]

1. Quoted in Bruna Nessif, "Katy Perry & John Mayer Unveil 'Who You Love' Cover Art—Take a Look!," Eonline.com, December 2, 2013. www.eonline.com/news/486732/katy-perry-john-mayer-unveil-who-you-love-cover-art-take-a-look.

2. Quoted in Taylor Weatherby, "John Mayer on How Katy Perry Relationship Inspired His New Music: 'Who Else Would I Be Thinking About?,'" *Billboard*, March 23, 2017. www.billboard.com/articles/columns/pop/7736443/john-mayer-interview-katy-perry-relationship-inspired-search-for-everything.

3. Quoted in Weatherby. "John Mayer on How Katy Perry Relationship Inspired His New Music."

such as from the website Consequence Of Sound: "*Prism* lacks the pop smash depth of *Teenage Dream*; it's unlikely we'll get six radio staples out of *Prism*. But, a solid three or four stereo-rattlers is not out of the question. While neither Perry nor *Prism* push any boundaries for pop music, they certainly raise bars."[78]

Perry continued the release of singles with "Dark Horse" on December 17, 2013, as the third official single from *Prism*. This song upheld the dark and moody aesthetic she had first predicted for the direction of her fourth album, yet in a different way. Perry described the song as "kind of witchy and dark, as if I was a witch warning this man not to fall in love with me, and if you do know I'm going to be your last."[79] The song presents more of an urban hip-hop sound, unlike most of her previous singles, and features rapper Juicy J.

## Moving On

One track on Perry's fourth album that held important significance for her was "By the Grace of God." This song detailed the emotional pain and struggle she went through after her divorce from Russell Brand in 2012. There was even a moment where she was so distressed over the ordeal she questioned if life was worth living anymore. The song's opening lyrics are about Perry lying on the bathroom floor contemplating her thoughts. Perry explained what it was like to create this song in an interview with *Billboard*:

> *['By the Grace of God'] is evident of how tough it really was at a certain point. I asked myself, 'Do I want to endure? Should I continue living?' ... I can only write autobiographically. I put all the evidence in the music. I tell my fans if they want to know the real truth about stuff, just listen to the songs.*[80]

Katy Perry eventually moved on after her divorce and began dating John Mayer.

# Starting Her Own Record Label

On June 17, 2014, Perry announced the start of her own record label, Metamorphosis Music, under Capitol Records. She signed Ferras as her first artist. So far, he has released one studio album titled *Aliens & Rainbows* in 2008. Perry praised the singer for his authentic way of approaching music and connecting with his audience:

> *Ferras is a man with a message, and a unique lyrical way of communicating his perspective on life that makes you feel connected to every note when you listen ... 'Speak in Tongues' is a song with raw emotional power that I wish I wrote. I believe he is going to be an important artist to watch unfold. I am SO ecstatic the world gets to hear his music now both online and on tour with me.*[1]

The label was later renamed Unsub Records. In 2016, the artist CYN, who released her debut single "Together" on July 14, 2017, signed with the label. In an interview, CYN said,

> *Working with Katy and her team is everything I could have wished for. Katy asks me questions like, 'Are you finding yourself through your art? Do you feel comfortable?' These are questions you pray for your label to ask. Katy's like my older song sister, a mentor who understands that I'm my best when I'm allowed to be myself.*[2]

1. Quoted in Emilee Lindner, "Katy Perry Starts Her Own Record Label and Reveals Her First Signee," MTV News, June 17, 2014. www.mtv.com/news/1848357/katy-perry-ferras-metamorphosis-music/.

2. Quoted in Sadie Bell, "CYN, Katy Perry's Latest Label Signee, Wants to Make Sincere Pop Music For You," *Billboard*, July 14, 2017. www.billboard.com/articles/columns/pop/7865983/cyn-katy-perry-label-together-sincere-pop.

The track "Legendary Lovers" was inspired by a new relationship that blossomed during the recording of the album with music artist John Mayer, who she began dating in the summer of 2012. He also co-wrote the song "Spiritual" and played guitar on the track "It Takes Two," which he also helped name, according to Perry.

## Prismatic World Tour

On May 7, 2014, Perry began her *Prismatic World Tour* in Belfast, Northern Ireland, to promote her fourth studio album, *Prism*. From there she traveled to England, Scotland, the United States, Canada, Mexico, Australia, New Zealand, other parts of Europe, Asia, and South America. The tour ended on October 18, 2015, in Alajuela, Costa Rica. The tour included around 150 shows, made more than $204.3 million, and was attended by almost 2 million people. Some of the supporting artists who joined the tour included Icona Pop, Capital Cities, Ferras, Kacey Musgraves, Tegan and Sara, Becky G, Betty Who, Tove Lo, Charli XCX, the Dolls, and Tinashe, among others. *Rolling Stone* wrote in a May 2014 review of Perry's London, England, tour stop:

Katy Perry is shown here flanked by several dancers while performing on her *Prismatic World Tour* in 2015.

*Perry's show is not so much a visual feast, but more like the visual equivalent of binge-eating. Divided into seven separate set-pieces, featuring every production gimmick in the book and cramming in almost as many costume changes as songs, it's like one of those blockbuster movies that you really need to see more than once in order to take everything in.*

The review added, "Loud, garish, camp and never less than uproariously entertaining, it's a show designed to conquer the planet."[81]

## Super Bowl Performance

During her *Prismatic World Tour*, Perry was offered one of the most prestigious opportunities a performer can receive—a chance to perform at the Super Bowl halftime show. After it was reported that the National Football League (NFL) had a shortlist, which included Coldplay, Rihanna, and Perry, they made the official announcement on November 23, 2014, that Perry was their final choice. The historic moment for Perry took place on February 1, 2015, at the University of Phoenix Stadium in Glendale, Arizona, for Super Bowl XLIX.

"We got to prepare for a whole month," Perry said. "Before I stepped on that stage ... at the Super Bowl I had done it over 40 times, so it was almost like I was so used to it—that's why people were saying that I looked so relaxed ... I overprepared myself and did a lot of prayer and meditation."[82]

Perry made her grand entrance singing "Roar" while wearing a dress adorned with flames and riding a giant gold lion through a sea of people who parted to make a pathway for her. Next, she jumped on stage to dance with acrobatic human chess pieces on a huge chessboard to go into her song "Dark Horse." Lenny Kravitz then joined her and began singing the intro to Perry's "I Kissed A Girl," with Perry joining him shortly after. Then, she hopped onto another stage to sing "Teenage Dream" and "California Gurls" with dancing sharks, beach balls, and backup dancers. Next, Missy Elliott appeared on the stage singing her hits

# Katy Keene

Katy Perry is known for her extravagant costumes—from her Egyptian attire in her "Dark Horse" video, leopard print jungle outfit in her "Roar" video, or the 1980s-inspired outfit from her "Last Friday Night (T.G.I.F.)" video, to so many more. However, *Archie* comic book character Katy Keene is known for her almost identical wardrobe, leading some to believe Perry borrowed her outfit ideas from the comic book character. Buzzfeed writer Aylin Zafar wrote about the discovery in an article in May 2014.

"I saw that a few months ago," Perry told *Rolling Stone* in reference to the Katy Keene comparison, "and the Internet is so crazy. Like, that's crazy! I want to go get an MRI right now and have them look inside me and make sure I'm not a comic! But what freaked me out about it is, we looked into it, and it turned out she has a sister who's a redhead. And my sister is a redhead!"[1]

1. Quoted in "Katy Perry: I Didn't Base My Life on an Archie Comics Character," *Rolling Stone*, August 11, 2014. www.rollingstone.com/music/news/katy-perry-i-didn-t-base-my-life-on-an-archie-comics-character-20140811.

"Get Ur Freak On," "Work It," and "Lose Control." Perry ended the night flying through the air on a shooting star platform while singing the inspirational song "Firework" with plenty of fireworks exploding around her.

In addition to performing at one of the most important events of the year, Perry also released *Katy Perry: The Prismatic World Tour* concert film. The film had its official premiere at Los Angeles' Theatre at the Ace Hotel on March 26, 2015. For the rest of her fans who were unable to make it to this exclusive premiere, the DVD, Blu-ray, and digital download became available on October 30. Perry was featured in two other documentaries that year, including *Katy Perry: Making of the Pepsi Super Bowl Halftime Show*, which showed her preparation for her Super Bowl halftime performance, and *Jeremy Scott: The People's Designer*, which is about the career of designer Jeremy Scott.

## Taylor Swift Feud

As Perry went through the process of recovering from her traumatic divorce, she trudged on, achieving significant milestones for her career. However, this popularity also came with its obstacles, such as the media making assumptions about her and competition with other artists. One of these artists was Taylor Swift, who is now known for having a well-known and ongoing "feud" with Perry.

Perry and Swift both began their musical careers around the same time in the early 2000s. At first, the pair seemed to outwardly support each other. In 2009, Swift gave Perry a compliment on Twitter: "Watching the Waking up in Vegas video," Swift wrote. "I love Katy Perry. I think I'm going to hang her poster on my wall now."[83] Perry responded with, "You're as sweet as pie! Let's write a song together about the subject we know best … for my new record. It'll be brilliant."[84] Needless to say, that song was never written. Then, in 2014, some controversy surrounding their friendship was mentioned in the media. In a *Rolling Stone* article, Swift made a pretty heavy accusation about a fellow female artist she refused to name; however, most believe it to be Perry: "For years, I was never sure if we were friends or not," Swift said. "She would come up to me at awards shows and say something and walk away, and I would think, 'Are we friends, or did she just give me the harshest insult of my life?'" Swift went on to explain exactly when she knew something was awry in their friendship:

> She did something so horrible … I was like, "Oh, we're just straight-up enemies." And it wasn't even about a guy! It had to do with business. She basically tried to sabotage an entire arena tour. She tried to hire a bunch of people out from under me. And I'm surprisingly nonconfrontational—you would not believe how

*much I hate conflict. So now I have to avoid her. It's awkward, and I don't like it.*[85]

In response to Swift's comments in *Rolling Stone*, Perry posted on Twitter: "Watch out for the Regina George in sheep's clothing."[86] Regina George is the mean, controlling, and deceiving character in the movie *Mean Girls*. In an interview with *Billboard*, when asked if the tweet was about Swift, Perry responded, "If somebody is trying to defame my character, you're going to hear about it."[87]

In 2014, Swift released the track "Bad Blood" from her album, *1989*. The song, which features the lyrics, "If you live like that, you live with ghosts,"[88] was supposedly aimed at Perry. Publications such as *Billboard*, *Rolling Stone*, *TIME*, and

When Katy Perry and Taylor Swift first met, they were big supporters of each other's music and talent.

*Washington Post* made the connection to Perry, as she has a song titled "Ghost" on her fourth album, *Prism*.

Even though Perry had some detractors, she still maintained a loyal fan base, and she did not let the negativity distract her from pushing forward. She continued on her journey of finding herself and welcomed the evolution in her career that was to come. Thus far, she was recognized as a pop queen in the industry, but she was yearning to go in a different direction.

# Chapter **Seven**

# Witness to Stardom

Over the years, Katy Perry has built a following of loyal fans, enchanting them with her numerous catchy pop songs. With popularity, however, comes criticism. For Perry's fifth album, she decided to move away from the upbeat pop sound, which served her well in the past, and instead explored new music genres. Changing her image so drastically was a risk for Perry, but as other successful artists have done before her, she wished to grow as a musician and public figure in new ways.

## *Taking a Break*

In October 2015, after touring on her *Prismatic World Tour* for two years straight, Perry went on a well-deserved hiatus to preserve energy and take care of her mental health. In an interview with

Katy Perry transformed her look in 2017 by cutting her hair short and dyeing it blonde.

*Access Hollywood* in February 2017, she spoke about her time spent during the hiatus, saying she learned how to cook, was able to spend more time with her nieces, and just simply live her life without the rigorous schedule she was accustomed to, being one of the busiest pop stars in the world. Perry said, "Mental health is really important, and like, there's a lot of pressure in this industry and in social media and all that stuff. You just got to take care of yourself or else you're going to just fall into pieces."[89]

In a February 2016 *New York Times* article, Perry revealed she was in the "research and development phase" of her fifth studio album, and disclosed no other specific information. "I've been going at it for eight or nine years in the spotlight, and then before that there's that decade of hustle that never gets recognized but still shows up in your wrinkles. So right now I'm taking a little time. I don't want to jump on any trends. I just need to evolve."[90] It was not until June 2016 that Perry began the songwriting process for her forthcoming album.

## Summer Olympics

Before releasing her fifth album, however, Perry released her song "Rise," on July 14, 2016, a song NBC chose to be used as the anthem for the 2016 Summer Olympic Games in Rio de Janeiro, Brazil. In a video message to her fans aired on the *Today* show, she expressed her excitement in releasing the track:

> There is ... a song that's been brewing inside of me for years, that has finally come to the surface. I was inspired to finish it now rather than save it for the album because ... now more than ever, there is a need for our world to unite. I know that together we can rise above fear—in our country, and around the world.[91]

The song received mixed reviews from critics, with the *New York Times* deeming the track "limp."[92] In another review, however, Chris Ingalls of Pop Matters said the song "works nicely"[93] as the theme song for the Olympics. Perry made the song available for streaming on Apple Music and for download on iTunes.

# **Orlando** Bloom

Another development that came out of 2016 for Perry was the relationship between her and actor Orlando Bloom. Romance rumors about the pair first began after they were spotted at two Golden Globe awards parties in January of that year. A source in March told *E! News* Perry and Bloom were an official couple. Throughout the rest of the year, they were seen together at events, such as the 2016 Met Gala and Democratic National Convention. They also enjoyed various vacations together in Hawai'i; Aspen, Colorado; Italy; and Shanghai Disneyland.

While their relationship seemed to be thriving, with engagement rumors on the rise in August 2016, the couple ended their relationship in February 2017. Bloom spoke of the couple's breakup to *Elle UK* in April 2017: "We're friends. It's good. We're all grown-up. She happens to be someone who is very visible, but I don't think anybody cares what I'm up to. Nor should they. It's between us. It's better to set an example for kids and show that [breakups] don't have to be about hate."[1]

The pair was later spotted together again, leading some to believe they had rekindled their romance. They were seen attending an Ed Sheeran concert in August 2017 and also spent Labor Day together that year.

1. Quoted in Rebecca Hawkes, "Orlando Bloom Speaks About Katy Perry Split: A Timeline of Their Relationship," *The Telegraph*, April 13, 2017. www.telegraph.co.uk/films/2016/11/23/orlando-bloom-katy-perry-timeline-relationship/.

## *Political Activism*

In the time spent between releasing her fourth and fifth album, Perry also devoted a large amount of time to endorsing Democratic presidential candidate Hillary Clinton during her 2016 campaign.

Katy Perry was very vocal in her support for Hillary Clinton during the 2016 presidential election.

Back in 2014, Perry mentioned how she wanted to write a Clinton campaign theme song for the former first lady, who had not yet announced her 2016 presidential run at that time.

After Clinton announced her run on April 12, 2015, Perry continued her support by performing at several major events to help promote Clinton's campaign, two of which included the "I'm With Her" fundraiser concert at Radio City Music Hall and the Democratic National Convention (DNC). Perry sang "Unconditionally" from her fourth album, *Prism*, at the "I'm With Her" event. She said of Clinton: "I sing this next song for her because I do believe this woman shows unconditional love."[94]

Before her performance at the DNC, Perry exclaimed, "I didn't finish high school and unfortunately I don't have a formal education but I do have an open mind and I have a voice. So I'm asking you to have an open mind and to use your voice ... on November 8." After singing "Rise," Perry let out an exuberant "Let's roar for Hillary,"[95] before singing "Roar."

When Perry found out Clinton had lost the 2016 election to Donald Trump, it was a huge letdown. Perry had been in New York City at what was supposed to be the official victory party for Clinton preparing to celebrate her win when she was hit with the news, a memory she refers to as "traumatizing."[96] She remembers grabbing Lady Gaga's hand and processing the news together.

## Purposeful Pop

As a sort of response to the election results, Perry decided to release the lead single from her fifth studio album, "Chained to the Rhythm," on February 10, 2017. After Trump won the election, the singer admits she was depressed about what was an unwanted outcome for her. Instead of writing her usual upbeat pop song, Perry poured her emotions into her new album, producing music unlike anything she had ever made before. Speaking with *Access Hollywood*, she explained the meaning behind her lead single: "The song is really meant to start conversations. It's meant to pose a question in our mind. I think if anybody is seeing what they're seeing and is still asleep or [unfeeling], I think that we all need to start listening to each other … We need to have conversations with both sides to be united."[97]

Describing her new album, Perry added a post on Twitter that read, "We gonna call this era Purposeful Pop,"[98] which led people to wonder what exactly this statement meant. "I've seen behind the curtain … and I can't go back," Perry told *Vogue* explaining her process of creating what she labels "purposeful pop." "I used to be the queen of innuendo [derogatory suggestions], everything done with a wink. Now I want to be the queen of subtext—which is a cousin to innuendo, but it's got more purpose."[99]

Australian singer-songwriter Sia, who is a seasoned artist in her own right, assisted Perry in writing "Chained to the Rhythm." The duo had previously worked together on the track "Double Rainbow," featured on *Prism*. "I've known her for years, I've known her my whole career in the spotlight, and we've seen each other at all these places and gone through ups and downs."[100] Another artist offering up his talents on the track is Skip Marley, Bob Marley's grandson. Marley also helped with writing the song, along with Max Martin and Ali Payami.

Reviewer Samantha Schnurr of *E! News* gave the song a favorable review: "Though the song sounds like a soon-to-be party classic with its easy pulse and disco elements, layered underneath

# **Family** Matters

During Katy Perry's therapy session with psychologist Siri Sat Nam Singh, which was part of her four-day YouTube live stream "Katy Perry Live: Witness World Wide," she revealed she participates in regular group therapy sessions with her family. Having grown up in a religious and somewhat sheltered household, Perry's curiosity pulled her away from that life and introduced her to the world outside of this lifestyle. Perry and her parents have experienced tension in their relationship in the past due to their opposing viewpoints and outlooks on life, but she credits their therapy sessions for helping them all to respect each other's opinions and to realize it is normal to not agree on everything:

*Our family time together is better than it's ever been ... There's been such a healing because of therapy and I'm so grateful for it. Even with our political time. So they believe one thing and I think one thing ... but it's OK. And I talk*

the upbeat veneer, Perry delivers a strong message about awareness and activism—and, according to her, how it's lacking."[101]

While the song received many good reviews, it peaked at only number 4 on the Billboard Hot 100. However, when the track was first released, it earned more than 3 million streams within 24 hours of its Spotify release. This allowed Perry to break the record for the highest amount of first-day streams for a single track by a female artist.

The next single released from Perry's fifth album was "Bon Appétit," which features the hip-hop group Migos. *NME* critic Jamie Milton called the song "a recipe for greatness" and the "supremely confident, addictive, steamed-up sound of summer 2017."[102] However, in another review of the song, *New York Times to them and sometimes it's hard to hear, but I still listen and they respect that ... And they listen to me because I've created a safe space for them as well. It's equal. So it's been amazing to be able to learn from my parents ... I almost feel like it was meant to be that way. Like I was meant to learn that lesson through my parents. That like it's not all one-sided ... That we have to speak with each other and not at each other.*[1]

Katy Perry is shown here at an event in 2016 with her father. She credits family therapy with improving their relationship.

1. "Katy Perry—Therapy Session (Witness World Wide)," DailyMotion video, 58:52, June 2017. www.dailymotion.com/video/x5q56an.

critic Jon Caramanica offered up his opinion: "Ms. Perry is in her least convincing mode—dance-floor diva—but the production is direct and effective."[103] The song did not appear very high on the Billboard Hot 100, landing at number 59.

## Reconciliation

Perry's third single "Swish Swish" incorporates house-inspired electronic dance music (EDM) and hip-hop sounds, which are experimental genres for Perry, who normally sticks with the pop music style. The song also features a rap verse by Nicki Minaj. In the comical music video for the track, Perry is seen playing on an uncoordinated, awkward basketball team facing against a team of physically fit, intimidating athletes. For most of the video, Perry's team is seen losing, but after witnessing a performance by Minaj and her band of confident dancers at halftime, Minaj transfers her confident energy to Perry. Finally, the team's luck changes, they prevail, and they start winning the game.

While the track only peaked at number 46 on the Billboard Hot 100 chart, there was also a significant amount of gossip surrounding Perry's intentions of releasing the track. The song has allegedly been recognized as a response to Swift's "Bad Blood," as Perry reportedly labels the former country singer a "sheep" in wolf's clothing in the lyric: "From a shellfish or a sheep, don't you come for me."[104] However, in a live-streamed conversation with Arianna Huffington to promote her latest album, Perry expressed she was ready to let the feud with Swift go: "I'm ready to let it go. Absolutely, 100 percent ... I forgive her, and I'm sorry for anything I ever did, and I hope the same from her, and I think it's actually ... I think it's time."[105]

## Witnessing Feedback

On June 9, 2017, *Witness* was released, and when the reviews came in, they were primarily on the negative side. In a review from the *Telegraph*, Neil McCormick criticized Perry's use of the phrase "purposeful pop" in relation to her new music: "That clunky phrase suggests a push towards higher artistic ground but turns out to mean pop that isn't really fit for the purpose ... the more time you spend with each song, the more it sounds like a variation on something you've heard done better before."[106] Pitchfork reviewer Jillian Mapes gives a little credit to Perry where it is due but overall gives it a bad rating: "On her fourth album, the pop superstar finds a more unifying sound but struggles to come up with lyrics that aren't plain cringe-worthy."[107]

One review that was on the more positive side came from *Entertainment Weekly*'s Kevin O'Donnell: "Proud girl-power moments ... course throughout much of *Witness*. And it's refreshing to hear Perry distance herself further from ... *Teenage Dream*."[108] However, it is far from a rave review.

## "Katy Perry Live: Witness World Wide"

To coincide with the release of her fifth album, Perry took part in a four-day YouTube live stream called "Katy Perry Live: Witness World Wide." The singer moved into a *Big Brother*-style house and was filmed for four days straight starting on June 8. The end of the stream concluded with a free concert for Perry's fans in Los Angeles on June 12.

During the course of the stream, she participated in a therapy session, meditated, and enjoyed visits from several special celebrity guests, such as RuPaul, Jesse Tyler Ferguson, Anna Kendrick, Sia, Neil deGrasse Tyson, James Corden, and Gordon Ramsay, among others. Some of the activities she participated in included doing yoga with Ferguson, playing truth-or-dare with Corden, and cooking with Ramsay.

The therapy session consisted of her speaking to psychologist Siri Sat Nam Singh. In the session, Perry covered topics such as her past battle with depression and suicidal thoughts following her divorce from Russell Brand in 2012. "I feel ashamed that I would have those thoughts, feel that low and that depressed,"[109] Perry said of that time period in her life. She also touched on how she has struggled with having to shift between the persona of Katy Perry and her true self, Katheryn Hudson, which is partly

During the "Katy Perry Live: Witness World Wide" stream, Katy Perry shared a lot of intimate moments with her fans.

# American *Idol*

Along with releasing her fourth album and embarking on a world tour, Perry joined the new version of *American Idol*. The other judges included were R&B singer Lionel Richie and country singer Luke Bryan. After accepting the first judge position for the comeback season of the show, Perry said,

> I am honored and thrilled to be the first judge bringing back the American Idol *tradition of making dreams come true for incredible talents with authentic personalities and real stories ...*
>
> I'm always listening to new music, and love discovering diamonds in the rough ... From mentoring young artists on my label, or highlighting new artists on my tours, I want to bring it back to the music.[1]

1. Quoted in Yvonne Villarreal, "Katy Perry Confirmed as Judge on ABC's 'American Idol,'" *Los Angeles Times*, June 1, 2017. www.latimes.com/entertainment/la-et-entertainment-news-updates-may-katy-perry-american-idol-1494967595-htmlstory.html.

the reason for her new hairstyle. She revealed one of the reasons for her short new blonde haircut was because she "didn't want to look like Katy Perry anymore."[110]

There were mixed responses to Perry's choice of promotion, as some labeled it a "bizarre publicity stunt,"[111] while others applauded her for her honesty and vulnerability. Sarah Daffy from the *Daily Telegraph* commented on the live stream: "It's refreshing to me that Katheryn doesn't completely have ... [it] ... together and that she's just given billions of people around the globe the opportunity to feel OK with not having ... [it] ... together too—even if only for a moment."[112]

# Witness *Tour*

In support of her fifth album, Perry kicked off *Witness: The Tour* on September 19 in Montreal, Canada. She played dates in North America, Europe, and the Oceania region. The tour consisted of elaborate stage sets, vibrant costumes, and intricately choreographed dance routines. Some highlights included Perry taking part in an oversized basketball game, performing while sitting atop a planet among a galaxy of stars, and singing while in a giant outstretched hand. She also wore a gown adorned in 30,000 Swarovski crystals while singing her hit song "Firework."

Once again, as the reviews for the tour rolled in, there were contrasting opinions, but for the most part, they were favorable with minor criticisms. *New York Times* critic Jon Caramanica said, "Katy Perry's 'Witness' tour highlighted the singer's approach to pop as ecstatic experience."[113] Reviewer Erica Bruce of the *Washington Times* praised Perry for making a personal connection with her audience despite the large arena setting the concert was housed in: "Perry's music can be called many things, but it always brings together an audience of many different colors, ages and genders—every one of them joyously singing their hearts out. To be witness to that joy is a special thing."[114]

As Perry continues to change as a music artist and a person, she will undoubtedly remain open with her fans. One constant has been her loyalty to her fans, and due to her allegiance to them, they have given her just as much, if not more, loyalty in return. Without her fans' support, there would be no reason for her to continue as a performer.

Despite all the adversity she has faced as an artist, she continues to put her best foot forward and succeeds. Hitting roadblocks and receiving criticism from the media are normal for Perry, but it has thickened her skin and made her a stronger individual. While she may struggle with her identity, between the persona of performer Katy Perry and Katy Hudson, the young girl who grew up in Santa Barbara, one thing is certain—she will never stop evolving.

# Notes

## Introduction: An Unconventional Pop Star

1.  Quoted in "A Play Date With Katy Perry," CBSNews.com, September 26, 2010. www.cbsnews.com/news/a-play-date-with-katy-perry/.

2.  Quoted in "'All Access': Katy Perry," CBSNews.com, February 4, 2009. www.cbsnews.com/news/all-access-katy-perry/.

## Chapter One: Sheltered Life to Cultural Exposure

3.  Quoted in Amy Spencer, "Katy Perry (She Kisses Boys, Too!)," *Glamour*, January 5, 2010. www.glamour.com/magazine/2010/01/katy-perry-she-kisses-boys-too.

4.  Quoted in "Find Out What Influences Katy Perry's Cute Style!," *Seventeen*, February 5, 2009. www.seventeen.com/fashion/celeb-fashion/news/a3706/katy-perry-fashion-qa-interview/.

5.  Quoted in Mike Burr, "Katy Perry: Interview," Prefix, February 6, 2008. www.prefixmag.com/features/katy-perry/interview/17027.

6.  Quoted in Burr, "Katy Perry: Interview."

7.  Quoted in Rob Sheffield, "Girl on Girl: Katy Perry," *Blender*, September 24, 2008, pp. 54–55.

8.  Quoted in Sheffield, "Girl on Girl," p. 55.

9.  Quoted in Sheffield, "Girl on Girl," p. 55.

10. Quoted in Jon Wilde, "I'm a Natural-Born Glamour Ninja—And I Like It: Katy Perry on Her Unique Style," *Mail Online*, July 21, 2009. www.dailymail.co.uk/home/moslive/article-1198292/Im-natural-born-glamour-ninja--I-like-Katy-Perry.html.

11. Quoted in Sheffield, "Girl on Girl," p. 54.

12. Quoted in "'All Access': Katy Perry."

13. Quoted in Leah Greenblatt, "Katy Perry's Long Road," *Entertainment Weekly*, July 25, 2008. ew.com/article/2008/07/25/katy-perrys-long-road/.

14. Quoted in James Montgomery, "Katy Perry Dishes on Her 'Long and Winding Road' from Singing Gospel to Kissing Girls," MTV. com, June 23, 2008. www.mtv.com/news/1589848/katy-perry-dishes-on-her-long-and-winding-road-from-singing-gospel-to-kissing-girls/.

15. Russ Breimeier, "Reviews/Music Review: Katy Hudson," *Christianity Today*, January 1, 2001. www.christianitytoday.com/ct/music/reviews/2001/katyhudson.html.

16. Tony Cummings, "Katy Hudson—Katy Hudson," Cross Rhythms, July 26, 2001. www.crossrhythms.co.uk/articles/42/p1.

17. Quoted in Greenblatt, "Katy Perry's Long Road."

18. Quoted in "'All Access': Katy Perry."

19. Quoted in "'All Access': Katy Perry."

20. Quoted in "'All Access': Katy Perry."

## Chapter Two: The Unpredictable Music Industry

21. Quoted in Gary Graff, "Interview: Katy Perry—Hot n Bold," *The Scotsman*, February 21, 2009. www.scotsman.com/lifestyle/interview-katy-perry-hot-n-bold-1-829754.

22. Quoted in Vanessa Grigoriadis, "Sex, God & Katy Perry," *Rolling Stone*, August 19, 2010. www.rollingstone.com/music/news/sex-god-katy-perry-rolling-stones-2010-cover-story-20110607.

23. Quoted in Greenblatt, "Katy Perry's Long Road."

24. Quoted in Sheffield, "Girl on Girl," p. 55.

25. Quoted in Sheffield, "Girl on Girl," p. 55.

26. Quoted in Greenblatt, "Katy Perry's Long Road."

27. Quoted in "'All Access': Katy Perry."

28. Quoted in Cortney Harding, "Katy Perry: Single Lady," *Billboard*, February 11, 2009. www.billboard.com/articles/news/269425/katy-perry-single-lady.

29. Quoted in Harding, "Single Lady."

30. Quoted in Sheffield, "Girl on Girl," p. 55.

31. Quoted in Sheffield, "Girl on Girl," p. 55.

32.  Quoted in Lewis Corner, "Katy Perry: Labels Wanted Me to Be Like Kelly Clarkson, Avril Lavigne," Digital Spy, May 22, 2012. www.digitalspy.com/music/news/a382978/katy-perry-labels-wanted-me-to-be-like-kelly-clarkson-avril-lavigne/.

33.  Quoted in Jan Blumentrath, "Interview with Chris Anokute," Hit Quarters, October 18, 2010. www.hitquarters.com/index.php3?page=intrview/opar/intrview_Chris_Anokute_Interview.html.

34.  Quoted in Blumentrath, "Interview with Chris Anokute."

35.  Quoted in Blumentrath, "Interview with Chris Anokute."

36.  Quoted in Blumentrath, "Interview with Chris Anokute."

37.  Quoted in Blumentrath, "Interview with Chris Anokute."

38.  Quoted in Lori Shube, "Katy Perry Talks About Her Impressions of Her Experiences in the Music Industry," *Guitar Girl Magazine*, April 6, 2013. guitargirlmag.com/news/katy-perry-talks-about-her-impressions-of-her-experiences-in-the-music-industry/.

39.  Quoted in Blumentrath, "Interview with Chris Anokute."

## Chapter Three: Finding Success in the Mainstream

40.  Quoted in Wilde, "I'm a Natural-Born Glamour Ninja—And I Like It."

41.  Quoted in Wilde, "I'm a Natural-Born Glamour Ninja—And I Like It."

42.  Quoted in Robyn Morris, "Singer Katy Perry Bursts onto the Set of 'The Young and the Restless' to Promote Her Debut Album," LAsThePlace.com, June 5, 2008. lastheplace.com/2008/06/05/singer-katy-perry-bursts-onto-the-set-of-the-young-and-the-restless-to-promote-her-debut-album/.

43.  Jon Caramanica, "Dependent, Independent, Metalcore, Emo: It's All Punk to Them," *New York Times*, July 28, 2008. www.nytimes.com/2008/07/28/arts/music/28warp.html.

44.  Quoted in Lisa Owings, *Katy Perry: Chart-Topping Superstar*. Minneapolis, MN: Essential Library, 2015, p. 40.

45.  Lizzie Ennever, "Katy Perry *One of the Boys* Review," BBC Music, September 22, 2008. www.bbc.co.uk/music/reviews/dv25.

46. Stacey Anderson, "Katy Perry 'One of the Boys,'" *Spin*, June 25, 2008. www.spin.com/reviews/katy-perry-one-boys-capitol.

47. Genevieve Koski, "Katy Perry: *One of the Boys*," AVClub, July 7, 2008. music.avclub.com/katy-perry-one-of-the-boys-1798204514.

48. Darren Harvey, "Katy Perry—*One of the Boys*," musicOMH, September 15, 2008. www.musicomh.com/reviews/albums/katy-perry-one-of-the-boys.

49. Jeff Giles, "Katy Perry: *One of the Boys*," Bullz-Eye.com, 2008. www.bullz-eye.com/cdreviews/giles/katy_perry-one_of_the_boys.htm.

50. Quoted in "Katy Perry: Girl Trouble," *Sunday Star Times*, October 24, 2008. www.stuff.co.nz/sunday-star-times/features/profiles/688815/Katy-Perry-Girl-trouble.

51. Alice Fisher, "So Much More than the Girl Next Door," *Observer*, June 13, 2009. www.theguardian.com/music/2009/jun/14/katy-perry-shepherds-bush-review.

## Chapter Four: Riding the Fame Wave

52. Quoted in Blumentrath, "Interview with Chris Anokute."

53. Quoted in Kimberly Dillon Summers, *Katy Perry: A Biography*. Santa Barbara, CA: ABC-CLIO, 2012, p. 22.

54. Quoted in "What's Behind Your Visual Transformation for *Teenage Dream*?," YouTube video, 2:52, posted by Katy Perry, November 8, 2010. www.youtube.com/watch?v=NL_NGRZFrdo.

55. Quoted in Blumentrath, "Interview with Chris Anokute."

56. Quoted in Blumentrath, "Interview with Chris Anokute."

57. Quoted in Tom Shone, "Katy Perry," *Guardian*, August 6, 2010. www.theguardian.com/music/2010/aug/07/katy-perry-interview.

58. Quoted in Shone, "Katy Perry."

59. Kitty Empire, "Katy Perry: *Teenage Dream*," *Observer*, August 21, 2010. www.theguardian.com/music/2010/aug/22/katy-perry-teenage-dream-review.

60. Chris Richards, "Album Review of *Teenage Dream* by Katy Perry," *Washington Post*, August 24, 2010. www.washingtonpost.com/wp-dyn/content/article/2010/08/23/AR2010082304256.html.

61. Rob Sheffield, "Katy Perry Teenage Dream," *Rolling Stone*, August 23, 2010. www.rollingstone.com/music/albumreviews/teenage-dream-20100823.

62. Quoted in Associated Press, "Katy Perry Leads All-Star Cast at 'VH1 Divas Salute the Troops,'" *Billboard*, December 5, 2010. www.billboard.com/articles/news/949737/katy-perry-leads-all-star-cast-at-vh1-divas-salute-the-troops.

## Chapter Five: Love, Loss, and Inspiration

63. Quoted in Carissa Rosenberg Tozzi, "Katy Perry," *Seventeen*, September 2010, p. 193.

64. Quoted in Tozzi, "Katy Perry," p. 183.

65. Quoted in Alison Prato, "Katy Perry Head over Heels," *Cosmopolitan*, November 2010, p. 38.

66. Quoted in ABC, *The View*, October 13, 2010. theview.abc.go.com/recap/wednesday-october-13-2010.

67. Katy Perry (@katyperry), Twitter, October 19, 2010, 2:03 p.m. twitter.com/katyperry/status/27868155212.

68. Quoted in Christina Garibaldi, "Katy Perry Says She 'Did Everything' to Save Her Marriage," MTV News, June 26, 2012. www.mtv.com/news/1688385/katy-perry-divorce-part-of-me-movie/.

69. Quoted in THR Staff, "THR Cover: Katy Perry on Russell Brand, the Media and Conversations with God: 'I Still Believe,'" *Hollywood Reporter*, June 20, 2012. www.hollywoodreporter.com/news/katy-perry-russell-brand-part-of-me-movie-divorce-339358.

70. Quoted in Jaclyn Hendricks, "Russell Brand was Living a Life He Detested While Married to Katy Perry," Page Six, October 28, 2015. pagesix.com/2015/10/28/russell-brand-slams-katy-perry-marriage-in-new-doc/.

71. Quoted in Garibaldi, "Katy Perry Says She 'Did Everything' to Save Her Marriage."

72. Quoted in Vicki Woods, "Beauty and the Beat: Katy Perry's First Vogue Cover," *Vogue*, June 20, 2013. www.vogue.com/article/beauty-and-the-beat-katy-perrys-first-vogue-cover.

## Chapter Six: Prismatic Epiphanies

73. Quoted in Matt Diehl, "Katy Perry's 'PRISM': The Billboard Cover Story," *Billboard*, September 27, 2013. www.billboard.com/articles/columns/pop-shop/5740580/katy-perrys-prism-the-billboard-cover-story.

74. Quoted in Diehl, "Katy Perry's 'PRISM.'"

75. Quoted in Diehl, "Katy Perry's 'PRISM.'"

76 Quoted in "Katy Perry Talks Inspiration Behind 'Unconditionally'/UNICEF," YouTube video, 2:05, posted by UNICEF. December 9, 2013. www.youtube.com/watch?v=D_W8vFeTSZ0.

77. Jason Lipshutz, "Katy Perry's 'PRISM': Track–By–Track Review," *Billboard*, October 21, 2013. www.billboard.com/articles/review/5763162/katy-perrys-prism-track-by-track-review.

78. Chris Bosman, "Katy Perry—Prism," Consequence of Sound, October 21, 2013. consequenceofsound.net/2013/10/album-review-katy-perry-prism/.

79. Quoted in Christina Garibaldi, "Katy Perry's 'Dark Horse' is a 'Warning,'" MTV News, August 28, 2013. www.mtv.com/news/1713269/katy-perry-dark-horse-prism/.

80. Quoted in Diehl, "Katy Perry's 'PRISM.'"

81. Daniel Kreps, "Katy Perry Preps 'Prismatic World Tour Live' Concert Film," *Rolling Stone*, August 31, 2015. www.rollingstone.com/music/news/katy-perry-preps-prismatic-world-tour-live-concert-film-20150831.

82. Quoted in Jon Blistein, "Katy Perry on Super Bowl: 'God Said, 'You Got This,'" *Rolling Stone*, February 8, 2015. www.rollingstone.com/music/news/katy-perry-on-super-bowl-god-said-you-got-this-20150208.

83. Quoted in Ruth Kinane, "Taylor Swift and Katy Perry: A Timeline of Their Feud," EW.com, August 27, 2017. ew.com/music/taylor-swift-katy-perry-timeline/july-2009.

84. Quoted in Kinane, "Taylor Swift and Katy Perry."

85. Quoted in Josh Eells, "The Reinvention of Taylor Swift," *Rolling Stone*, September 8, 2014. www.rollingstone.com/music/features/taylor-swift-1989-cover-story-20140908.

86. Quoted in Jackie Willis, "Katy Perry Confirms 'Mean Girls' Tweet was Aimed at Taylor Swift," Etonline.com, January 30, 2015. www.etonline.com/music/158932_katy_perry_says_mean_girls_tweet_was_about_taylor_swift.

87. Quoted in *Billboard* Staff, "Katy Perry Comments on Her Infamous 'Mean Girls' Tweet," *Billboard*, January 30, 2015. www.billboard.com/articles/columns/pop-shop/6457915/katy-perry-talks-mean-girls-tweet?utm_source=twitter.

88. Taylor Swift, "Bad Blood," Big Machine. Originally released May 17, 2015.

## Chapter Seven: Witness to Stardom

89. "Grammys 2017: Katy Perry on the Meaning Behind 'Chained To The Rhythm,'" *Access Hollywood*, February 12, 2017. www.accesshollywood.com/videos/grammys-2017-katy-perry-on-the-meaning-behind-chained-to-the-rhythm/.

90. Quoted in Joe Coscarelli, "Katy Perry on Grammy Parties, a New Album and Keeping Calm Online," *New York Times*, February 11, 2016. www.nytimes.com/2016/02/12/arts/music/katy-perry-grammy-awards-party.html.

91. Quoted in Khalea Underwood, "Katy Perry Releases First New Song Since 2013," *Us Weekly*, July 15, 2016. www.usmagazine.com/entertainment/news/katy-perry-releases-new-song-for-olympics-video-w429360/.

92. Jon Pareles, Ben Ratliff, and Jon Caramanica, "The Playlist: Katy Perry's Limp Olympics Anthem and Justice's Grooving Return," *New York Times*, July 15, 2016. www.nytimes.com/2016/07/16/arts/music/playlist-katy-perry-rise-justice.html.

93. Pop Matters Staff, "Katy Perry—'Rise' (Singles Going Steady)," PopMatters, August 22, 2016. www.popmatters.com/post/katy-perry-rise-singles-going-steady/.

94. Quoted in Matthew Claiborne, "Katy Perry, Elton John Perform at Hillary Clinton Fundraiser In New York," ABC News, March 3, 2016. abcnews.go.com/Politics/katy-perry-elton-john-perform-hillary-clinton-fundraiser/story?id=37359679.

95. Quoted in Sarah Grant, "Watch Katy Perry 'Rise' and 'Roar' for Hillary Clinton at DNC," *Rolling Stone*, July 28, 2016. www.rollingstone.com/politics/news/watch-katy-perry-rise-and-roar-for-hillary-clinton-at-dnc-w431537.

96. Quoted in Caryn Ganz, "Katy Perry Woke Up. She Wants to Tell You All About It," *New York Times*, June 14, 2017. www.nytimes.com/2017/06/14/arts/music/katy-perry-witness-interview.html.

97. "Grammys 2017: Katy Perry on the Meaning Behind 'Chained To The Rhythm," *Access Hollywood*.

98. Quoted in Spencer Kornhaber, "Katy Perry Proclaims a New Era of 'Purposeful Pop,'" *Atlantic*, February 10, 2017. www.theatlantic.com/entertainment/archive/2017/02/katy-perry-chained-to-the-rhythm-purposeful-pop-trump/516264/.

99. Quoted in Hamish Bowles, "Katy Perry Is Leaving Her Cutesy Style Behind and Going Androgynous, Architectural, and Political," *Vogue*, April 13, 2017. www.vogue.com/article/katy-perry-interview-religion-childhood-may-vogue-cover.

100. Quoted in Alicia Adejobi, "Chained To The Rhythm Helped Katy Perry's 'Depression' After Donald Trump Won US Election," Ibtimes.com, February 22, 2017. amp.ibtimes.co.uk/chained-rhythm-helped-katy-perrys-depression-after-donald-trump-won-us-election-1607925.

101. Samantha Schnurr, "Katy Perry's New Single 'Chained to the Rhythm' Will Have You Dancing Into the Weekend With a Message," Eonline.com, February 10, 2017. www.eonline.com/news/828188/katy-perry-s-new-single-chained-to-the-rhythm-will-have-you-dancing-into-the-weekend-with-a-message.

102. Jamie Milton, "Katy Perry and Migos' Sex-obsessed 'Bon Appétit' is a Recipe for Greatness," NME.com, April 28, 2017. www.nme.com/blogs/nme-blogs/katy-perry-migos-bon-appetit-review-2061813.

103. Jon Pareles, Jon Caramanica, and Giovanni Russonello, "The Playlist: Katy Perry and Haim Reach for New Flavors," *New York Times*, April 28, 2017. www.nytimes.com/2017/04/28/arts/music/playlist-katy-perry-haim-dj-khaled.html.

104. Katy Perry, "Swish Swish," Capitol. Originally released May 19, 2017.

105. Quoted in Jennifer Drysdale, "Katy Perry Says She's '100 Percent' Ready to 'Let Go' of Taylor Swift Feud: 'I Want the Best For Her," Etonline.com, June 10, 2017. www.etonline.com/news/219413_katy_perry_says_she_100_percent_ready_to_let_go_of_taylor_swift_feud_i_want_the_best_for_her.

106. Neil McCormick, "This is Pop that is Not Fit for Purpose—Katy Perry, Witness, Review," *Telegraph*, June 9, 2017. www.telegraph.co.uk/music/what-to-listen-to/katy-perry-witness-album-review/.

107. Jillian Mapes, "Katy Perry—*Witness*," Pitchfork.com, June 14, 2017. pitchfork.com/reviews/albums/katy-perry-witness/.

108. Kevin O'Donnell, "Katy Perry is Reflective, Anxious and Fired Up on Witness: EW Review," *Entertainment Weekly*, June 8, 2017. ew.com/music/2017/06/08/katy-perry-witness-review/.

109. Quoted in Laura Beck, "In a Very Emotional Livestream, Katy Perry Discussed Past Suicidal Thoughts," *Cosmopolitan*, June 10, 2017. www.cosmopolitan.com/entertainment/celebs/a10005049/katy-perry-worldwide-witness-livestream/.

110. Quoted in Beck, "In a Very Emotional Livestream."

111. Quoted in Joey Pucino, "Katy Perry Broadcasts Her Life via YouTube Livestream," *Sydney Morning Herald*, June 12, 2017. www.smh.com.au/entertainment/music/katy-perry-broadcasts-her-life-via-youtube-livestream-20170611-gwp42d.html.

112. Sarah Daffy, "Katy Perry's Committed the Dirtiest Celebrity Crime—She Chose to be Honest," *Daily Telegraph*, June 12, 2017. www.dailytelegraph.com.au/rendezview/katy-perrys-committed-the-dirtiest-celebrity-crime-she-chose-to-be-honest/news-story/171a312789ed96a2d2e56afb2c8b8e0e.

113. Jon Caramanica, "Review: Katy Perry, Queen of Froth, Stars in a Carnival of Her Own," *New York Times*, October 3, 2017. www.nytimes.com/2017/10/03/arts/music/katy-perry-witness-tour-review.html.

114. Erica Bruce, "Perry Brings her 'Roar' to Capitol One Arena," *Washington Times*, September 27, 2017. www.washingtontimes.com/news/2017/sep/27/concert-review-katy-perry-witness-stop-dc-appeals-/.

# Katy Perry Year by Year

## 1984
Katheryn Elizabeth Hudson is born on October 25 in Santa Barbara, California.

## 1993
Perry begins singing in her church choir.

## 1997
Perry shows a strong talent for music and receives her first guitar as a birthday gift.

## 1999
Determined to pursue a career in music, Perry drops out of high school and passes the General Educational Development (GED) test.

## 2000
Perry catches the attention of a group of musicians in Nashville, Tennesee, who agree to work with her and help her enter the music business.

## 2001
Red Hill Records releases Perry's first album, titled *Katy Hudson*. The company goes bankrupt at the end of the year.

## 2002
Perry auditions for Glen Ballard, who then invites her to move to Los Angeles, California, to try to launch her music career.

## 2003-2004
To avoid being confused with actress Kate Hudson, Katy changes her last name to Perry.

## 2004

Production team the Matrix invites her to be the lead singer for a new group they are forming; only weeks before the album's release, the project is canceled.

## 2005

Perry prepares to release a new album with Island Def Jam Music Group, but the company cancels the project; Perry goes to work on a solo album for Columbia Records; and Perry records videos for "Diamonds" and for "Simple," which is picked up for the soundtrack for the film *The Sisterhood of the Traveling Pants*.

## 2006

Columbia Records cancels Perry's album; Perry provides vocals and makes a video appearance in the single "Goodbye for Now" on the album *Testify* by P.O.D.; and Perry appears in videos for the songs "Cupid's Chokehold" by Gym Class Heroes and "Learn to Fly" by Carbon Leaf.

## 2007

Chris Anokute of Capitol Records convinces his company to sign Perry to a new contract; late in the year, "Ur So Gay" is released as a single for download, and Perry begins dating Travis McCoy of Gym Class Heroes.

## 2008

Perry provides vocals and a makes a video appearance in the single "Starstrukk" for the album *Want* by 3OH!3; Perry travels with the Vans Warped Tour; Capitol Records launches her album *One of the Boys*, which lands on Billboard's Top 200 chart at number 9; Perry sings "I Kissed a Girl" on *So You Think You Can Dance*; Perry records videos for "Hot n Cold," "I Kissed a Girl," and "Waking Up in Vegas;" her song "Fingerprints" is picked up for the movie *Baby Mama*; she appears as herself on the television show *Wildfire*, singing in a nightclub; Perry is featured on *The Young and the Restless*, portraying herself in a photo shoot; and Perry ends relationship with Travis McCoy.

## 2009

Capitol Records releases the album *Katy Perry: MTV Unplugged*; Perry adds vocals and a video appearance to the single "If We Ever Meet Again" for the album *Shock Value II* by Timbaland; her song "Hot n Cold" is added to the movies *The Proposal* and *The Ugly Truth*; "Hot n Cold" is sung by the Chipettes in the movie *Alvin and the Chipmunks: The Squeakquel*; Perry meets comedian Russell Brand while filming a cameo for the movie *Get Him to the Greek*; and on New Year's Eve, the couple becomes engaged.

## 2010

Perry's album that was recorded with the Matrix is revived and released as *The Matrix* by Let's Hear It Records; Perry records videos for the songs "California Gurls," "Firework," and "Teenage Dream"; Capitol Records releases her album *Teenage Dream*; the movie *When in Rome* picks up Perry's song "If You Can Afford Me" as well as "Starstrukk;" Perry appears in a music video for *When in Rome* performing "Starstrukk" with 3OH!3; Perry kicks off the new season of *Saturday Night Live* by singing "California Gurls" and "Teenage Dream;" she marries Russell Brand at a private ceremony in India; she performs at the American Music Awards; her new line of perfume, Kitty Purry, is launched; she appears on *The Simpsons*; "California Gurls" is ranked as the most-downloaded single in 2010 with 4.4 million downloads; and she is nominated for a Best Female Pop Vocal Performance Grammy Award for "Hot n Cold."

## 2011

Perry embarks on her world tour, *California Dreams*; Perry is featured in the movie *The Smurfs* as the voice of Smurfette; sales of *Teenage Dream* reach 1 million copies, earning Perry a platinum album award; "Firework" is played during the *Miss America Pageant*; Russell Brand asks Katy Perry for a divorce on New Year's Eve via text message; and Perry is nominated for four Grammy Awards: Best Pop Collaboration with Vocals for "California Gurls," Best Female Pop Vocal Performance for "Teenage Dream," and Best Pop Vocal Album and Album of the Year for *Teenage Dream*.

## 2012

Perry releases her biopic *Katy Perry: Part of Me*; Perry and Brand's divorce is finalized; Perry puts out a reissue of *Teenage Dream* titled *Teenage Dream: The Complete Confection*; Perry enters the studio to start working on her fourth studio album *Prism*; she starts dating John Mayer; and she is nominated for two Grammy Awards for Best Pop Solo Performance and Record of the Year for "Firework."

## 2013

Perry reprises her voice role as Smurfette in *The Smurfs 2*; she embarks on a humanitarian trip to Madagascar, Africa, with UNICEF; Perry and John Mayer release the duet "Who You Love," included on Mayer's sixth album, *Paradise Valley*; she debuts "Roar," the first single off of *Prism* in August; she releases her fourth studio album, *Prism*, in October; she releases "Unconditionally" as the second single off *Prism*; she releases "Dark Horse" as the third single off of *Prism*; and she is nominated for the Best Pop Solo Performance Grammy Award for "Wide Awake."

## 2014

Perry starts own record label; kicks off *Prismatic World Tour*; and is nominated for the Song of the Year Grammy for "Roar."

## 2015

Perry performs at the Super Bowl XLIX halftime show; premieres *Katy Perry: The Prismatic World Tour* concert film; performs at the "I'm With Her" fundraiser concert at Radio City Music Hall and the Democratic National Convention in support of Hillary Clinton; ends relationship with John Mayer; and is nominated for two Grammy Awards for Best Pop Vocal Album for *Prism* and Best Pop Duo/Group Performance for "Dark Horse."

## 2016

Perry begins the songwriting process for her fifth studio album; "Rise" is used as the anthem for the 2016 Summer Olympic Games; and Perry starts dating Orlando Bloom.

## 2017

Perry releases her fifth album, *Witness*; takes part in a four-day YouTube live stream called "Katy Perry Live: Witness World Wide;" and kicks off *Witness: The Tour*.

# For More Information

**Books**

Berry, Jo. *Katy Perry: California Gurl*. London, UK: Orion Books, 2011.
This book gives an inside look into Katy Perry's life and career, her upbringing in Santa Barbara, California, her success in the music business, her marriage to Russell Brand, and more.

Dickinson, Stephanie E. *Katy Perry*. New York, NY: Cavendish Square Publishing, 2015.
This book features an in-depth look at how Katy Perry achieved success on and off the stage as a successful singer and businesswoman.

Friedlander, Noam. *Katy Perry*. New York, NY: Sterling, 2012.
Friedlander's book is a detailed volume chronicling Katy Perry's rise to fame and transformation from Christian choir girl to pop sensation.

Heatley, Michael. *Katy Perry: The Ultimate Pop Princess*. Broomall, PA: Mason Crest, 2015.
This captivating book about Katy Perry's life, which includes eye-catching photographs, covers her rise to pop stardom and all the prestigious awards she has won along the way.

Hudson, Alice. *Katy Perry: Rebel Dreamer*. London, UK: Flame Tree, 2012.
This unofficial biography of Katy Perry delves into the singer's music career, elaborate outfits, life events, various opinions, and popular social media following.

## Websites

### Katy Perry Official Website
(www.katyperry.com)
This website, which is maintained by Katy Perry, includes photos, videos, news, schedules, merchandise, and links to her social media websites.

### Katy Perry on Facebook
(www.facebook.com/katyperry/)
This website is Katy Perry's official Facebook page where she connects with fans and notifies them of upcoming tour dates, events, and new music.

### Katy Perry on Instagram
(www.instagram.com/katyperry/)
Katy Perry's official Instagram page is where she connects with fans through posting personal photos.

### Katy Perry on Twitter
(twitter.com/katyperry)
Katy Perry's official Twitter page allows her to connect with her fans through short posts and links. She gives updates on tour information, appearances, music news, and other life events.

### *Rolling Stone*: Katy Perry
(www.rollingstone.com/music/artists/katy-perry)
This section of *Rolling Stone*'s website provides all the articles published by the magazine that mention Katy Perry.

# Index

# Picture Credits

# About the Author

**Vanessa Oswald** is an experienced freelance writer and editor who has written pieces for publications based in New York City and the Western New York area, which include *Resource* magazine, *The Public*, *Auxiliary* magazine, and *Niagara Gazette*. In her spare time, she enjoys dancing, traveling, reading, snowboarding, and attending many live concerts.